Connecting to the Gospel
Texts, Sermons, Commentaries

JAMES BOYD WHITE

WIPF & STOCK · Eugene, Oregon

CONNECTING TO THE GOSPEL
Texts, Sermons, Commentaries

Copyright © 2010 James Boyd White. All rights reserved. Except for brief quotations in critical publications or reviews, no part of this book may be reproduced in any manner without prior written permission from the publisher. Write: Permissions, Wipf & Stock, 199 W. 8th Ave., Suite 3, Eugene, OR 97401.

Wipf & Stock
An Imprint of Wipf and Stock Publishers
199 W. 8th Ave., Suite 3
Eugene, OR 97401
www.wipfandstock.com

ISBN: 978-1-60899-135-8

Manufactured in the U.S.A.

Unless otherwise indicated, all Scripture quotations are from New Revised Standard Version Bible, copyright © 1989 National Council of the Churches of Christ in the United States of America. Used by permission. All rights reserved.

To Mary

"Lord, how can man preach thy eternall word?"

—George Herbert, "The Windows"

Contents

Foreword by Walter Brueggemann | ix
Preface | xiii
Acknowledgments | xv

Introduction | 1

1. "Love One Another as I Have Loved You" | 9
2. Nicodemus | 15
3. Lazarus and the Rich Man | 22
4. Doubting Thomas | 29
5. Walking on Water | 38
6. The Good Samaritan | 45
7. The Narrow Door | 52
8. The Passion According to John | 58
9. The Parable of the Sower | 68
10. "Get Thee Behind Me, Satan!" | 75
11. The Laborers in the Vineyard | 82
12. The Transfiguration of Jesus | 89
13. Saturday Time | 94
14. Sending Out the Twelve | 99
15. "To Whom Can We Go?" | 105
16. "Prepare the Way of the Lord" | 112
17. Jesus on the Beach | 119

| 18 | Sending the Seventy | 126
| 19 | "Sell Your Possessions" | 133
| 20 | The Lost Sheep, The Lost Coin | 140
| 21 | The Pharisee and the Tax Collector | 148
| 22 | The Good Shepherd | 155
| 23 | "You in Me, and I in You" | 162
| 24 | The Mustard Seed | 168
| 25 | "Who Do You Say I Am?" | 176
| 26 | "Seventy Times Seven" | 182
| 27 | Healing the Leper | 189
| 28 | The Grain of Wheat | 196
| 29 | The Resurrection of Jesus | 202

Table of Gospel Readings | 209

Foreword

There are as many ways to preach as there are preachers; or perhaps there are as many ways to preach as there are sermons. The nature of a sermon remains elusive and enigmatic, and we only know that the Church cannot live without them. For the most part, preachers cannot quite say what they are doing in a sermon or how they do it. Good sermons are like the way in which a Supreme Court justice once characterized a less wholesome mode of communication, "You know it when you see it."

In the midst of that elusiveness, I commend with great enthusiasm the sermons of Jim White in this volume. It is possible that some readers of this volume will not know Jim White or the splendid academic career he has had. He is a faculty member at the University of Michigan in literature and in law, and he has spent his life learning to read texts well. He reads well all sorts of texts—the classics, court opinions, notes left on refrigerator doors, or whatever falls into his ready hand. He is a shrewd, discerning reader who sees in all its thickness what goes on in a text. He is also a teacher who is skilled at bringing his students along with him in the reading in persuasive, compelling ways, as is evident here in the introductions and concluding reflections that he offers for each sermon.

Happily White is also an Episcopal lay preacher who has practiced his reading art on biblical texts, and has learned to move the text along toward the sermon so that the text becomes a text for the whole of the Church. Unlike many preachers, White can say, with some precision and under some discipline, what he is doing in a sermon. His effort, every time, is to make a haunting connection between the biblical text and the ordinary way in which we live our daily lives. The connection he makes is never flat or obvious or one-dimensional; it is, rather, a haunting, by which I mean one is never quite fully sure of the connection and he leaves us always with something to chew on and reflect upon and decide. He does not do our work for us, but sets the table with rich resources for our continuing work. He knows that our soul work is not completed, but can be continued in trust and with joy.

Readers of these sermons will see that he does the task of connecting with probes and wonderments that are genuinely his own, but which he knows are ours as well, even if we have not yet recognized them as such. He knows that the preacher has no compelling authority other than being a credible witness to the truth that is beyond our control. He knows, moreover, that admonition or strong moral urging is counterproductive. Indeed, I suspect that his refusal to claim any authority for himself and his refusal to be didactic are congruent both with his personal style of life and with the shape of his own faith.

He sees, and in these sermons shows, that authentic Gospel faith is a challenge and a perplexity not only for novices in the faith but for those who know the story long and well. He sees exactly, as the old hymn has it, that those who know the story best "seem hungering and thirsting to hear it like the rest." Such sermons do reach out for new folk who are bewildered by how we talk in the church; but those grounded in faith also want it told again, fresh.

In these sermons, White is a compelling master of telling it again, fresh. He focuses here on the narratives from the Gospel readings that appear in the common lectionary. Characteristically, as he retells the old, old story, new challenges emerge from the narrative account and new questions are raised that pertain to ordinary life. White has a way to show how it is that we ourselves, we listeners, are like Dives, or Nicodemus, or Thomas, or the dozens of others whom he lines out for us. He understands that for many of these characters and for us, the issue is not lack of faith; it is rather resistance to or reluctance about the faith that they themselves already have, and the faith that we already have. It would be easier if it were a move from faith to unfaith, but the requirement is to process the faith that is already there, which is too daunting or too risky or too demanding . . . even when it is the faith we confess.

Along with his uncommon artistry, White's sermons bear recurring marks that make them such welcome offers:

—This preacher is pastoral and gentle. He has a patient, grace-filled awareness of how ordinary people live ordinary lives but also have the sense that something is missing in their daily lives. He invites probes about that something, and then he empowers us to make a change that will allow that something to enter and reshape our lives.

—This preacher marks his utterance by understated wisdom. One has the sense that one is hearing from one who has probed deeply and thought well and has seen how the dots connect in an alternative life. He puts his disciplined imagination to making hunches about what is going on in the text, which is very likely what is going on in our lives. He lets the characters of the story move out to a full life. Thus Nicodemus, at the end, circles around so that the narrative shows him bringing costly gifts, his new belief letting him break with his self-sufficient way in the world. And Thomas, after being left out and desolate, is on his way, joyously, to India. As White probes these characters, he details carefully what they exhibit of their lives that may also be a disclosure about our life in Christ.

—But alongside pastoral gentleness and alongside wisdom, White never fails to show how "disturbing" is the claim of the narrative, how it shows an alternative way that stands over against our old habits, and leaves us, from the moment of hearing, restless and dissatisfied with our old way of life. His artistry moves regularly toward a bite that does not leave us safe or unaffected.

Sometimes White soars with rhetoric that envelops us. Here are two such flights taken at random:

> The love of which Jesus speaks is not a program or a decision or a strategy or an obligation, but a felt commitment of the whole being—like the love in fact you feel for your child or spouse. It is real love; a movement of the whole heart, made in faith and hope and trust; a movement that is hobbled and crippled by any attempt to rationalize it, to structure it, to control it. (Chapter 6)

> Terrible things do happen in the world and will continue to do so. That will not stop. We should like it to but it won't. Jesus came back not to eliminate evil but to give us the capacity to live out of hope in a world with a great deal of despair; to live out of faith in a world with a great deal of denial; to live out of love in a world with a great deal of hate. (Chapter 17)

One might want to say "Amen." Better, "Wow." Or "Thank you Jesus!" The invitation and disturbance and surprise never end in this book.

In Atlanta on Saturday nights, H. Johnson, a disc jockey on NPR, offers each week a long, long program of wonderful jazz. Every Saturday night, in my time of listening, he never failed to play, not always back-to-back, two renditions of the same piece by Errol Garner. H. Johnson always introduced these renditions by saying, "Errol walked into a studio and sat down to play, and this is how he played it that time." One always noticed, as Johnson intended, that each performance was very different, depending on the imaginative freedom of the performer. A test case for White is his offer of two very different sermons on the same Passion narrative from the Gospel of John. (See chapters 8 and 13, below.) Not unlike Garner, White stepped into the studio (pulpit) and played it this way. How different each time! His imaginative rendering, each time, is a surprise, even though we know the plotline. It is a surprise because White is ready and able to put his immense imagination into the service of Gospel truth. As we follow along his twists and turns of variation in a story we know well, we can see that the preacher knows all about us, about our half-failed lives and our readiness for an alternative from which we cringe in fear and resistance. White knows all about us, because he lets us see that the text and the truth given in the text know all about us, and do not give up on us. White is, in the end, a preacher of hope. And when we hear, we may hope as well. He keeps coming back to the Resurrection of Jesus; he ends his final sermon here this way:

> So it is with the Resurrection. It changes life from the inside out. Now our every act, our every effort, has meaning, the meaning that comes from reciprocal love; our love for him, his love for us. He is life itself. His Resurrection is his and our victory over Death. Amen. (Chapter 29)

It is by such preaching that the church lives the news entrusted to it. Thank God for such preaching!

Walter Brueggemann
Professor of Old Testament, emeritus
Columbia Theological Seminary

Preface

THIS BOOK IS BASED on my own experience of religious life, especially as expressed in a series of sermons I have given as a lay preacher in the Episcopal Church, some of which are reproduced here, along with the Gospel texts they address. This is not a scholarly book, nor is it confessional in nature or a defense of the beliefs out of which it arises. It is not addressed to the world at large, but to those within the Church, or those interested in possibly becoming part of the life of the Church, for whom these texts are both foundational and problematic. It is an effort to represent my own engagement with the Gospel texts I discuss and my own attempt to understand the life to which they call me and other Christians.

My hope is that this book may be found useful by individuals or groups who are interested in the study of the Bible and what it means. My idea is that readers will work through the Gospel passages and take my sermons simply as starting points for thought and discussion, as examples of someone else doing the same thing, with whose efforts their own can be compared.

I am an Episcopalian but I hope that what I say can be heard and responded to by people in the other branches of Christ's Church.

Acknowledgments

I WANT HERE TO thank those who have helped me work to a position from which it was possible to give these sermons: my wife Mary, above all, whose constant love and confidence have been a wonderful and essential gift; Bishop Wendell Gibbs, who authorized my training as a preacher and licensed me as a lay preacher in the Diocese of Michigan; Bishop Robert Gepert, who gave me permission to preach at the Church of the Mediator in the Diocese of Western Michigan; the Rev. Harry Cook, who taught my preacher's class, and the other students too; Bernadette Pelland, my wise and kind spiritual director for many years; the Rev. John Nieman and the Rev. Alan Gibson, rectors of St. Andrew's Church, and the Rev. Paula Durren, the rector of the Church of the Mediator (the two churches where most of these sermons were preached), all of whom have been greatly supportive; the late Rev. John Crocker and the late Rev. Malcolm Strachan, both powerful influences in my boyhood; Joseph Vining, with whom I have shared these sermons and talked about the issues they raise; the Rev. John McCausland, with whom I have for several years exchanged sermons, to my great pleasure and benefit; Jefferson Powell, who generously read the whole manuscript with care and offered me much wise advice; Ann Chih Lin, Laura Florence, Mary White, and the Rev. Philip Dinwiddie, with whom I have worked for years on reading and thinking about the Bible; the Greek reading groups at St. Clare's Church and St. Andrews Church; James Bos, my teacher of biblical Hebrew, who has taught me much about the Hebrew Bible; and Walter Brueggemann, for support and wise counsel, and for his wonderful Foreword too.

Introduction

Learning to read the Gospel, and to connect it to one's life, is a central activity in the Christian life, from beginning to end. It is in a sense the foundation of the entire Church, for this is where we hear of Jesus of Nazareth, of his conversations with his disciples and others, of his life, death, and Resurrection. We never stop trying to tune ourselves to the Gospel, to learn from it. This is a challenge for a whole life, because the Gospel does not offer a set of clear rules or other statements that can serve as firm and safe stopping places in the confusions of our existence, but almost the opposite: it is a set of perplexing puzzles and problems and difficulties that invite engagement of the whole mind, the whole self, in a process of transformation, from the center out, which never ends.

Despite the way they are sometimes spoken of, the four Gospels (which together we call "the Gospel") are thus not cozy, sentimental, easy, or comfortable texts but deeply problematic. That is in a sense their point: to disturb and upset us; to shake us out of the values and attitudes that our culture has established within us or that we have made for ourselves; to change our sense of ourselves and our world, and our place within it; to give us a new set of motives and hopes. The Gospels call for a reorientation that will lead to a different sense of the nature and purpose of human life itself—and not just life in general, but our own actual lives, our own ways of being in the world.

Think of Jesus' central commands: to love God with all our minds and hearts and souls; to love our neighbor as ourselves; to love one another as he loves us. None of us does these things or can do them. Yet they are the center of Christian faith and ethics. What are we to do in the face of this impossibility?

This book is an effort to read and connect with the Gospel in a way that makes the process visible, in slow motion as it were. Not that what I do is in any way a model; rather it is simply one person trying to do what we all try to do, offered as an effort with which the reader can compare his or her own.

In form the book consists of a series of passages from the Gospels, each of which was part of the lectionary prescribed by the Episcopal Church for a particular Sunday. Each passage is preceded by a brief introduction, often with some questions, and is followed by the sermon that I gave on that text as a lay preacher, itself followed by a brief commentary. The arrangement is chronological in the sense that it begins with my first sermon and ends with some of my more recent ones. Obviously the important texts here are the Gospel passages; everything else is meant simply to open them up for thought and response.

The Gospel passages that appear here are, as I say, the texts that I was assigned in the order in which I was given them, not chosen or arranged thematically or historically. This may seem a disorderly way to proceed. Why not begin with Mark, the earliest, and end with John, the latest? Why not focus on the structure and meaning of each of the Gospels as a whole, explaining its purposes and how it seeks to achieve them? Why not pursue one theme across all the Gospels?

My answer is that this is not how we live with the Gospels in our collective life in liturgy and worship or, for the most part, in our individual lives either. My idea of the structure of this book it that should reflect the way we experience the Gospels in our actual lives, one short passage after another, each presenting its own difficulties of understanding, its own problems—often serious—for the person who wishes to connect the Gospel to his or her own life.

Think for example of the way in which most people find themselves caught up in the life of the Church. Very few people I think come to church for the first time because they are persuaded by abstract argument that the truths of Christianity are indeed true. In our lives outside the Church we do sometimes talk about such questions as the Existence of God, the Authority of the Church, maybe the Historicity of the Gospels, but I do not think these discussions lead many people to go to church.

What more often brings a person in the door is a confused and inarticulate sense of need, a desire for something perceived to be missing in life as it is ordinarily lived. This sense can be occasioned by many things: by the death of a friend or family member; by release from what had seemed like a mortal disease; by coming to know a person who seems more deeply alive than other people, and wanting to be with him or her, in the hope that some of it will rub off; by experiencing the birth of a child, the miraculous event in which there is suddenly present in the world another human soul, another source of meaning and experience; or maybe by what feels like simple curiosity but probably has much deeper roots than that suggests.

Despite the great variety of ways in which people are led into the Church and its life, I think there is something that almost all newcomers share: a sense that they do not quite know what is happening in the church they are attending or what it means; and a sense of confusion, even embarrassment at the oddity of their situation—what *am* I doing here? Often the new person is afraid, or shy, or feels vulnerable to criticism, including from his or her own logical and practical mind: "You can't possibly believe this stuff: Why are you here?" He or she is likely to be awkward, ignorant, unsure about many things, among them both the central tenets of the Church's system of belief and the meaning of the holy texts, perhaps especially the Gospels.

The way a particular church typically addresses such a person is not by trying to explain everything in clear and rational terms, which cannot be done, but by welcoming the person into the experience of the place. This experience itself will probably seem rather haphazard and random: you are exposed bit by bit to liturgy, to scripture, to prayer, to various sacred days and rites, to the social relations that bind the congregation together, to the feelings of belonging and hope and caring that seem to surround you. You are joining a community that has a life of its own, its own way of doing things—with a history that in some sense goes back two thousand years—and you are plunged right into the middle of that life, that history. The process is not orderly or rational. It is experiential. You may find that it is deeply important to be part of it, and still feel that in a profound way it does not make sense. Or you may not like what you see, and go away.

If you do keep on, in time you will gradually come to understand something of what is happening, just as you learn a language in a foreign country. You will learn what others do in the liturgy or other service, and what you are to do as well—when to stand, when to kneel, when to look at the prayer book, if there is one, or at the hymnal or other book of sacred songs. You will know what to say and to sing, and bit by bit it will begin to make some sort of sense. You gradually find your bearings. You may start to use this language first to ask questions and think about possible responses to them, then to define your own place in the world and your own hopes for your life. If all goes well, you will find that this world takes on meaning, in an ever deeper way.

But it is likely that understanding at an explicit level, theological understanding, will still seem to elude you, and of course you will never understand all that you wish you could. Reading helps, but there is a sense in which abstract reasoning about God and the Gospels and the Church is only thinly connected, if at all, to the actual experience of the life to which you are being exposed.

How then are we to think about what we are doing, what we are learning? This is a lasting and difficult question, and one to which this book is addressed. For most people the answer lies in their own experience: as they read the Gospel texts or hear them read, and try to expound them or hear them expounded, they find themselves more and more at home with a certain kind of thinking and of life—including a certain kind of criticism, doubt, and argument. This process, however, like the whole life of the Church, is not intellectually ordered in a coherent way—say from the general to the specific, or from first things to last things, or by other categories of thought or experience. It is all jumbled up, one thing after another, and learned all at once, as I say, like a language. That has at least been my own experience.

The aim of this book is offer you as the reader, in slow motion as it were, an encapsulated version of the experience of learning to understand, and to use, the fundamental language of the Christian Church, particularly as it derives from the Gospels. My thought is that the experience of working through these Gospel passages, and comparing your own responses with my own, might help prepare you for the real experience of joining a church or make more intelligible the experiences of church life that you may have already had.

I hope it is not too surprising to be told that most of what I say about the life of the person discovering the Church, and beginning to live on its terms, is true of all of us in the Church, even the most experienced. For we are all on the edge of understanding; we all face doubt and mystery; we all are in one sense beginners, starting again in what we hope is a fresh way every day of our lives.

As a friend once wrote to me, all of the Christian life, from the first glimmer of interest to the death of the greatest saint, is a process of learning to read the Gospel and trying to find ways to connect it with our lives. We are always disciples, we are always learners. The Gospel is not so much a resting place stocked with answers as an invitation to engage in a process by which our life will be transformed, from the inside out, through and through. By definition such a challenge can never be met fully in this life.

So this book is addressed not just to those on the edge of the Church, at the first stages of discovery, but also to those who have thought about these matters for a long time and lived with the puzzles and problems they present. We are all engaged in a life of change and growth we cannot wholly understand. We are all learning how to connect our selves and lives with the Gospel.

In the sermons reproduced below I am myself trying to learn how to read the Gospels, and how to think about them, especially in connection with ordinary experience of our own time and place. If you are merely curious, or your interest in theology and the life of the Church has barely begun, I hope that you can take this as a piece of the life you might experience if you continued on. Indeed, I hope that you can think of this is an invitation to do just that—if only because you find yourself disagreeing with what I say in these sermons or thinking that they are simply inadequate to the task they have set themselves.

Likewise, if you have deep familiarity with the texts, and have lived with them long, I hope that too you will find it of value to read and think about them once more, and compare your own responses with what I say. In doing this, I hope you retain some of the anxieties of a person new to the Church, for these feelings are entirely appropriate to the task of the life we have before us, whatever our preparation may have been.

As a person of long experience with the Gospel texts you may of course find yourself judging and criticizing what I say, and, as I say above, that would not be a bad thing but a good one. Such critical responses and disagreements would in fact be important engagements in the very life to which I think the Gospels call us, which should certainly be a life of intellectual and moral responsibility for what we say, for what we believe, and for what we do.

Naturally in the course of this work a series of important theological questions arise. What I say about them is the best I can manage, based on my own experience and thought, as a lay person engaged with these texts. I am not an expert. I do not apologize for this, because I think Christian theology in the end must have its life in the minds and hearts of ordinary people struggling with the Gospels, with the tradition of the Church, and with their own experience. There is a sense in which the Gospels themselves have their real life, today, in the way we engage with them, individually and collectively. For me this is where theology too has its life, in our own engagements with its questions, and here I represent my own version of that activity.

There are a lot of specific issues, many of them debated fiercely, that I simply do not address. Who actually wrote each of the Gospels, out of what prior materials, with what agenda or bias? What connection is there between what appears in the Gospels and what actually happened in the life of the historical Jesus of Nazareth? Are the Gospel stories factually true? Do they faithfully record in Greek what Jesus said in Aramaic, and, if that is what we think, how can that possibly be? How should each Gospel be understood as a complete text, with a shape and structure of its own, meant to address a particular historical context? By whom, and in what process, were the four Gospels that we now use selected as authoritative? To what editing have they been subjected? Are the Gospels in fact the foundation of the Church, as I earlier said, or is the Church the foundation of the Gospels?

These are all questions to which scholars have devoted enormous energies. As an historical and intellectual matter they are of course of real interest. But they are not questions for the preacher, or at least not for me in that role. I have accepted the Gospels as they have come down to us, and as they are read in our liturgies and other services, for these are the texts upon which our common life is based. I assume for the most part that the English translation is effective, though occasionally I look to the Greek for clarification.

I am asking a different set of questions from the ones listed above. At bottom they are these. How can we connect to the Gospel passage we have read? What sense can we make of it, in the context of our own lives? What sense of difficulty, what sense of truth, can we bring from it to our own experience? How can we build our lives upon it, both as individuals and as a community of Christians?

In speaking to these issues I try to be as honest as I possibly can. I make this perhaps unnecessary remark because of a striking experience I had when I first gave a sermon (which I did from notes, not a written text). I knew I had a life of doubt as well as faith and I was anxious about whether my doubts disqualified me from presuming to preach a sermon. When I stood before the congregation, and silence fell upon the room, I suddenly felt as though a bright light from heaven shone down upon me, telling me, not in words but in fact, that I simply must speak the truth, whatever it might be. I was not to protect myself with evasions, but to say the truth as it was given me to speak it, at any price whatever. Honesty had become a sacred and absolute duty. Fortunately, the truth I discovered was that, when put to it in that way, my deepest beliefs were and are rather orthodox. But I did not know that until this happened.

These sermons are the work of a lay preacher, not a priest or other ordained minister. This means, among other things, that I do not speak as a pastor to my congregation, guiding, prodding, reflecting on our common life. They are not pieces of a continuing conversation of the kind that a pastor has with his parish, developing its own set of themes and allusions, with its own past and future. I am not a stranger to the parish, of course; I know my fellow parishioners and they know me; but I am not their priest or pastor. Accordingly my sermons are more strictly text based than sermons often are—less addressed to current social or moral issues, less about the life of the parish and the larger world—and more directly focused on the question whether, and how, we can connect with the Gospel passage that is our reading for the week.

A further word about the sermons. In the 1990s I was occasionally asked by the rector of St. Clare's Church in Ann Arbor to give a sermon, as part of a general movement to involve the laity more fully in the liturgy. Perhaps I gave a sermon every two or three years. I loved doing it, and when our diocese offered a course for lay preachers, I leapt at the chance. After a year and a half of training I was certified as a lay preacher, in 2001. Since that time I have given one or two sermons a year at St. Andrew's Church in Ann Arbor, which is now my home church. In addition, I have given several sermons each year at the Church of the Mediator, a small church in the Diocese of Western Michigan near the place where we have spent our summers and now spend an increasing part of the rest of the year.

The sermons that follow appear, with slight editing, in the form in which they were presented, except for the first three, which were not read but delivered from notes, many years ago, and which therefore I have had to write out for the first time. I have selected the sermons that I thought most useful for the purposes of this book, arranged in the order in which they were given. The comments that follow each sermon are meant to complicate any sense of completeness or finality that might otherwise be created by the fact that the sermon comes to a kind of conclusion, as sermons must of necessity do, and to open up further questions or lines of thought that might be useful to the reader, either working alone or in a discussion group.

My idea is that this book can be read slowly, perhaps best one unit at a time, and that the reader's own puzzles and responses can be taken as part of the experience it offers. If you approach these passages this way, you will be doing theology of an important kind. I hope you will find by the end that you have a way of thinking about these passages and the life of the Church that is your own.

Unless otherwise indicated, the passages from the Bible are all from the New Revised Standard Version, used with permission.

1

"Love One Another as I Have Loved You"

Our first Gospel text, immediately below, seems at first to be an easy and comfortable one, even for someone who is full of doubt and uncertainty as to his or her own beliefs, for in it Jesus simply commands his disciples to love one another—surely an ideal that most of us share.

But is this text more difficult and challenging than that? How are we to understand what Jesus is really saying here, and how are we to respond to it?

The Gospel of John 15:9–17

"As the Father has loved me, so I have loved you; abide in my love. If you keep my commandments, you will abide in my love, just as I have kept my Father's commandments and abide in his love. I have said these things to you that my joy may be in you, and that your joy may be complete.

"This is my commandment, that you love one another as I have loved you. No one has greater love than this, to lay down one's life for one's friends. You are my friends if you do what I command you. I do not call you servants any longer because the servant does not know what the master is doing; but I have called you friends, because I have made known to you everything I have learned from my Father. You did not choose me, but I chose you. And I appointed you to go and bear fruit, fruit that will last, so that the Father will give you whatever you ask him in my name. I am giving you these commands so that you may love one another."

ST. CLARE'S CHURCH, MAY 5, 1991

May the words of my mouth and the meditations of my heart be always acceptable in thy sight, O Lord, my strength and my redeemer.

THE PASSAGE WE HAVE just read contains one of the most important and beautiful of all the utterances of Jesus: *"This is my commandment, that you love one another as I have loved you."* This is his command to his disciples and to us. In a sense it is the center of his teaching as the Gospel of John presents it.

For me this is a comfortable passage, and I imagine the same may be true for you as well. It is echoed in the famous passage from John's first letter: "Beloved, let us love one another, because love is from God; everyone who loves is born of God and knows God" (1 John 4:7).

The idea that God is love, that we are to love one another as he loves us, is a reassuring and familiar one. We can connect this idea of God with the love we experience in our homes, among our friends, and in our church—the actual love we bear for others, and the better love we aspire to. We may not be quite so sure about other images of God in the Old Testament and the New, but the idea that God is love seems deeply right and deeply comfortable.

God is love. How right and true.

But perhaps this is too easy, too comfortable. Is this all there is to it? The more we say "God is Love" the more it sounds like a Hallmark card.

One place to start might be the word *love* itself. What does Jesus mean by it? Of what kind of love is he speaking?

"As the Father has loved me, so I have loved you." This sounds wonderful: to be loved as the Father loves the Son. But how did the Father in fact love Jesus? He sent him to live among us and to die a hideous and shameful death as a criminal. Is that how Jesus loves us? Is this how we are to love one another? To send each other to death?

"This is my commandment, that you should love one another as I have loved you." Again this sounds wonderful at first, but then we remember how Jesus in fact loved us: he chose freely to die for us. Is this the kind of

love we are to have for each other? The implication that this is what Jesus means is made explicit when he tells us, *"No one has greater love than this, to lay down one's life for one's friends."*

It is clear that the kind of love of which Jesus speaks is not love as we normally use the term: not love as good will, or affection, or mutual support, or even mutual blessing. It is not the kind of love most of us know.

It is love as the willing acceptance of suffering and death for another. It is love as sacrifice.

So Jesus' command turns out not to be comfortable at all, but deeply threatening. It calls for a kind of love of which none of us is fully capable. Jesus calls upon us not merely to love one another—that in some sense we surely do—but to love one another as he loves us, and that we surely do not.

Jesus makes things still worse when he adds: *"If you keep my commandments, you will abide in my love."* This suggests the obvious question: "And if not?" There is a dreadful unstated threat there, as Jesus has just made plain in an earlier part of his speech: *"Whoever does not abide in me is thrown away like a branch and withers; such branches are gathered, thrown into the fire, and burned"* (John 15:6).

All this suggests a far more serious and troubling view of what "love" means in Jesus' commandment than we originally thought. The kind of love we are to have for one another is the love that enables us to die for each other or, perhaps worse, to send each other to die for the sake of others. And if we fail in this superhuman task, we are to be thrown into the fire and burned.

It turns out that this passage is not a confirmation of what we already do and are, not an easy assurance of support, but a call to an utterly radical and impossible change: to a kind of love that involves a transformation of all that we are, to a giving of the self in sacrifice. Of this kind of love I know that I at least am not capable. I think very few people are.

It may help us see what Jesus is really asking here if we think about what it would mean if we were in fact to love one another in the dangerous way that he commands, if we were, in some real sense, to lay down our lives for our friends and neighbors. I think it would produce something unimaginable: a revolution in feeling and conduct and thought that would change everything.

Suppose we really did regard every child born in Detroit, or Bangkok, or Darfur, as being wholly as valuable, as precious, as our own children—as equally deserving of, and entitled to, all the support and nourishment necessary for their full development. What would that mean? Or if we thought of every aged person, alone in a hospital or hospice, or house or apartment or hut, of whatever race or nation or people they might be, as being as valuable as ourselves? Or if we thought of our students and patients and customers, the people on the bus or the train or in the airport—or on the street, or in prison, or sick and dying—all as members of the same human family, each equally deserving of love and joy and happiness? Not as players in a game of competition, which some win and some lose, but all as the object of ultimate concern? Jesus is telling us that we are to consider the needs of every person in the world as equal in importance to our own.

He of course is right. Every single baby born into the world rightly knows, deep in soul and body, that he or she should be loved. Every baby knows, too, what that love should consist of: not a sentimental adoration, not a merger of feeling or self, but the sense that the child is ultimately valuable, wholly precious; the conviction that nothing is more important than his or her healthy growth into maturity; and the readiness to experience deep joy in his or her presence—joy expressed in smiles and laughter and talk and play—as well as the deepest caring. Every child born into the world is born ready to receive love, and to return it—at first as an infant, but in the end, if properly loved, as a loving parent in his or her own right. And this kind of love, as every parent knows, means not only joy, but self-sacrifice.

Jesus is thus saying what we in a sense already know, what everyone already knows: that each human being is a soul, a center of value, equal in this respect to every other human being, and that every human action, or system of social relations, that reduces any person to the control of others, that treats any person as an object of force or manipulation, is unjust and evil.

If the people to whom Jesus is speaking—including us, now, today, in this room—begin to hear him and try to become what he is calling them to be, they, and we, will always be on the margin of the world, in a community apart. In a profound way the task that Jesus defines in his great commandment sets them, and us, against every system of power in world—for every system of power dehumanizes and trivializes the weak, the poor, the abandoned.

Jesus' followers may be a tiny group, a dozen men in an upper room, but it is their duty, and the duty of each of us, to act on Jesus' view of the world and its people, even when no one else does. This is so even if it means that we will be exposed to the hostility and destructiveness of the same forces that killed Jesus. This can be dangerous indeed: tradition tells us that each of the apostles, except John, died violently at the hands of others.

All this is wonderful but very hard. Perhaps the hardest question the passage presents is this: What are we to do about the fact that we cannot, we simply cannot, achieve this revolution in ourselves? We can try, but we know that we are not capable of universal and unconditional love, and never will be. How then are we to come to terms with our own frailty, weakness, incapacity? Our own selfishness?

I do not have an answer to that question, but I do think it is addressed here, not so much in this particular passage as in the Gospel as a whole—in the whole story of Jesus' arrival among us, his life with us, and his death on the cross.

For in this story we are shown that God—the Father and the Son—love us in an astonishingly self-sacrificing way, with just the kind of love of which we are incapable.

It is our own inadequacy, our radical self-centeredness, that calls forth this love, a love that sets a standard by which we are all the more inadequate. We are told to imitate Jesus, and we try, but we will always fail.

The true miracle is that we know, in our very inadequacy, that we are loved. Jesus Christ died to save sinners, including those—all of us—who cannot love as he would have us do.

We cannot reciprocate his love, which is beyond our capacity, but we can recognize it and respond to it.

As Jesus says at the end, all of this depends not upon our choice, but his: *"You did not choose me, but I chose you."* For which let us offer our thanks to God.

Amen

This passage from John is part of a long series of speeches, or maybe one immensely long speech, that Jesus gave to his followers the night before his death, often called The Farewell Discourse. What Jesus says here is highly repetitive and deeply urgent. Some people find it verbose, even boring, but for me it is wonderful, full of the sense that Jesus knows that this is the last time he will be able to talk to his friends and is trying to say it all, or at least the most important things, trying to give his friends something they can keep with them after he is gone. I think this explains the repetition and the urgency, and something else too, the sense that the speech is full of deep love for his friends—an actual performance of the kind of love he commands them to have for each other.

At the end of the passage Jesus says to them, and to us, "*I have appointed you to bear fruit, fruit that will last.*" What does this mean for us? What is the "fruit" he speaks of? Can we bear fruit that will last?

2

Nicodemus

This passage tells the story of Nicodemus, the Pharisee, who comes to Jesus in the night to say he knows that Jesus is sent from God. Jesus' response is remarkable: he is not at all grateful, as Nicodemus may have expected, but critical, mysterious, confusing, even rejecting.

Why does Jesus talk that way to this earnest person who seems to want to follow him? What is Nicodemus' response to what Jesus says, and what are we to make of it?

Where are *we* in this story?

The Gospel of John 3:1–16

Now there was a Pharisee named Nicodemus, a leader of the Jews. He came Jesus by night and said to him, "Rabbi, we know that you are a teacher who has come from God; for no one can do these signs that you do apart from the presence of God."

Jesus answered him, "Very truly, I tell you, no one can see the kingdom of God without being born from above." Nicodemus said to him, "How can anyone be born after having grown old? Can one enter a second time into the mother's womb and be born?"

Jesus answered, "Very truly, I tell you, no one can enter the kingdom of God without being born of water and Spirit. What is born of the flesh is flesh, and what is born of the Spirit is spirit. Do not be astonished that I said to you, 'You must be born from above.' The wind blows where it chooses, and you hear the sound of it, but you do not know where it comes from or where it goes. So it is with everyone who is born of the Spirit."

Nicodemus said to him, "How can these things be?"

Jesus answered him, "Are you a teacher of Israel, and yet you do not understand these things? Very truly, I tell you, we speak of what we know and testify to what we have seen; yet you do not receive our testimony. If I tell you about earthly things and you do not believe, how can you believe if I tell you about heavenly things? No one has ascended into heaven except the one who descended from heaven, the Son of Man. And just as Moses lifted up the serpent in the wilderness, so must the Son of Man be lifted up, that whoever believes in him may have eternal life.

"For God so loved the world that he gave his only Son, so that everyone who believes in him may not perish but may have eternal life."

St. Clare's Church, March 7, 1993

May the words of my mouth and the meditations of my heart be always acceptable in thy sight, O Lord, my strength and my redeemer.

This Gospel passage has some of the most beautiful inspiring and mysterious language in the New Testament. Many things could be said about it, but I want to think of it today as a story, and to do so from the point of view of Nicodemus himself. I will be asking you to imagine yourself into the story, asking what all this looks like to him.

The first thing we need to know about Nicodemus is that he is a Pharisee. The Pharisees get a bad name in the New Testament, but, as we are often told, this is not entirely fair. The Pharisees were serious reformers of Judaism at a time when it was under internal and external threat. They were committed to maintaining their institutions and their religion through adherence to its ancient practices. To them Jesus must have seemed like a wild and dangerous person, popular among the poor and outcast—a demagogue and a potential destroyer of Judaism.

If I imagine my own response to a twenty-first century prophet who appeared on the scene and claimed to make our religion new, and in doing so attracted a wide following, I can easily imagine myself responding like a Pharisee, full of fear and condemnation and with a sense of my own righteousness as well. Nicodemus the Pharisee is in this way like me—and maybe like you.

He is like me, and maybe like you, in another respect as well, namely, that he comes to Jesus "in the night" to tell him that he knows that Jesus is a teacher sent from God.

Why do you suppose he comes in the nighttime? I suspect it is because he wants to be able to tell Jesus that he knows who he really is, but does not want to pay the price of doing so. He wants to acknowledge the truth, but does not want his friends to know what he is doing, because before them he would be ashamed. He wants to be a secret or private adherent of Jesus. I think most of us know what that is like.

A third respect in which Nicodemus is like you and me is the nature of the question that he has been pursuing. For when he tells Jesus, "We know you are a teacher from God," it means that he has been asking himself the question, "Who is this Jesus? Is he a teacher from God?"

That is his question, and it is a question for all of us.

Nicodemus' instinct is to look for an empirical or logical answer to his question, one that will meet the demands of the rational mind. Thus it is that he says, in effect: "We know you are a teacher from God because you do these miracles. No one could do miracles if he did not have God on his side; you do miracles; and therefore God is on your side."

This approach is a familiar one, for we too often speak and act as though the questions—Who is Jesus? Is he sent from God?—could be answered in a logical or empirical way. Sometimes we may think that it would be wonderful if we had some miracles as proof upon which we could rely, as Nicodemus does. But we don't seem to have them. We cannot point to our own experience of Jesus healing the blind or the lame as proof with which to convince our doubting selves or our doubting friends. We may even feel a little cheated that the age of miracles seems to be over.

So this is our Nicodemus. He is one of us. He says to Jesus in the night, in effect, "We know you are a teacher from God because you have done these miracles." He waits for a response. I think he expects Jesus to express some satisfaction and pleasure that such an important person as

Nicodemus acknowledges his nature and his role. But that is not what Jesus says to Nicodemus, not at all.

Instead, what Jesus says seems to come from nowhere. *"Very truly, I tell you no one can see the kingdom of God without being born from above."* Actually the Greek word that is here translated "from above" can also mean "again," and this is the sense in which Nicodemus takes it, responding in his practical-minded way, by asking in essence: "How can that be? Can an old man enter again his mother's womb?" He is a learned man, and he likes to answer a question with a question.

To this question Jesus comes back harder than before: *"No one can enter the kingdom of God without being born of water and Spirit"*—born, that is, not a second time but in a different and unimaginable way. This must have been mystifying to Nicodemus in the extreme, and what Jesus says next does not help: *"The wind blows where it chooses, and you hear the sound of it, but you do not know where it comes from or where it goes. So it is with everyone who is born of the Spirit."* When Nicodemus expresses confusion, Jesus says to him: *"Are you a teacher of Israel, and yet you do not understand these things?"*

Nicodemus must be completely perplexed. He thought he was coming to Jesus, really as a kind of favor and with real risk to himself, to tell him, "I know who you are and understand you and honor you." But Jesus seems to rebuff him, rejecting both his attempt to ingratiate himself and his empirical mode of thought and proof.

Perhaps Jesus answers this way in part because Nicodemus has indicated that the miracles are the ground of his belief. If so, Jesus is resisting the idea that miracles can serve as the kind of proof Nicodemus wants. And to us he is saying that we should not lament it if we do not have miracles upon which to base our faith.

But Jesus did do miracles, lots of them, and if they are not to be the ground of faith, as Nicodemus seems to think, what is their proper place in Jesus' ministry? I think Jesus is saying here something like this: "The miracles are not done as a kind of proof of my power or identity, but as a way of getting your attention. Now that I have it, I want you to listen to the real thing, which is: *'The wind blows where it chooses, and you hear the sound of it, but you do not know where it comes from or where it goes.'"* The real thing—the presence of God—is a mystery, certainly not subject to comprehension or proof by empirical or rational means.

The truth of God *is* a mystery. It is not physical or material, nor can it be established by empirical proof or logical demonstration. This truth is fluid and alive, like water or air. It is like wind, or spirit. You do not see it but it is real. You can feel it on your face but you cannot see it.

Perhaps you know someone who is deeply alive in his or her spirit, someone who seems full of wisdom and grace. In such a person there is often something like the wind, coming and going. We do not understand it exactly, but we know it is there. There is something beautiful and good, something flowing from him or her to us.

Jesus is telling Nicodemus that it is not the miracle that counts, not the transformation of water into wine, or the healing of the blind man, but the inner transformation of the soul. This is what he means when he bluntly tells Nicodemus, *"You do not receive our testimony."* Nicodemus, he is saying, has not experienced the essential transformation of which Jesus speaks. He must be devastated to be told such a thing.

After this Nicodemus seems to be completely forgotten, both by Jesus and by John. Jesus talks a bit about Moses and the serpent, then concludes with the famous summary statement, *"God so loved the world that he gave his only Son, so that whoever believes in him may not perish but may have everlasting life."* This is a wonderful statement of promise and hope, but Nicodemus is just not there, even as audience. He has in fact just been told that he is not one who believes, so the promise does not reach him.

But it turns out that he reappears twice in John's Gospel, both times significantly. The first time is at the moment when Jesus has come to Jerusalem and is preaching in the Temple. Jesus has greatly aroused the people, who are listening and responding to him. The Pharisees, clustered together, don't quite know what to do. They and the chief priests send the Temple police to arrest Jesus, but the police come back without him.

The Pharisees and priests upbraid the police, contemptuously asking, "Surely you have not been deceived too, have you? Has any one of the authorities or of the Pharisees believed in him?" (John 7:47–48).

Nicodemus is present. This is his moment. He could say, "*I do. I believe.*" But he does not. Yet he does do something. He asks, "Our law does not judge people without first giving them a hearing to find out what they are doing, does it?" That is, can't we give Jesus a hearing and at least learn what he says in his own defense? Here Nicodemus the lawyer is insisting upon procedural regularity. This is much safer than confessing belief, but it is still dangerous, as the Pharisees make clear when they turn to him and say, "Surely you are not also from Galilee, are you?" The threat is plain. Nicodemus has stood up for Jesus and begins to see what it might cost him.

Near the end of the whole story, Jesus' body is taken down from the cross, to be prepared for burial. John tells us this: "Nicodemus, who had first come to Jesus by night, also came, bringing a mixture of myrrh and aloes, weighing about a hundred pounds" (John 19:39).

I find this moving beyond words. The one who half sees it, thinks he gets it, wants to know, doesn't know, doesn't get it, goes by night, not by day, who can't stand up among his friends and say "I believe," but can think of legalistic protections for Jesus, this person—so much like me, so much like you—comes at the end with spices to anoint the body. And not just some spices, but way, way too much, a hundred pounds of aloe and myrrh!

This is not someone seeking empirical proof where it cannot exist, but a person who has made a commitment of his soul. The transformation that Jesus spoke about, of being born again or born from above, which made no sense at the time, has actually happened to Nicodemus. An internal miracle has occurred that makes external miracles unnecessary.

This miracle is the capacity for love and devotion that Jesus inspired in him. The gift of spices and ointments is its expression in the world. Nicodemus represents every person who is troubled by the thought of who Jesus is; who cannot bring himself really to accept him; who cannot bring himself really to reject him; but who, in the most important way, perhaps without ever having language for it, joins him and his people. He stands for all of us.

Nicodemus brought the spices on Good Friday, or perhaps the day after. He did not know it but there awaited him, on Sunday, the greatest miracle of all.

Amen

In our culture we regularly hear the phrase "born-again Christian," often said in a dismissive way. But Jesus here uses the image of birth—of rebirth or birth from above—with great seriousness.

What happens when we try to use this language in our own lives, of ourselves? Have *we* been born again, or born from above? How do we know, and what does it mean?

3

Lazarus and the Rich Man

The next passage is a parable told by Jesus, apparently to his disciples and the Pharisees (who have just been described by Luke as "lovers of money"). It is the story of Lazarus: not the famous one, in John, the brother of Martha and Mary who is raised from the dead, but an important one nonetheless. This Lazarus is a beggar who dies, and goes to heaven; Dives, the traditional name for the rich man in story, has done nothing to help Lazarus in life and now finds himself after death in a place of torment. What happens to him there, and why?

Where are we in this story?

The Gospel of Luke 16:19–31

"There was a rich man who was dressed in purple and fine linen and who feasted sumptuously every day. And at his gate lay a poor man named Lazarus, covered with sores, who longed to satisfy his hunger with what fell from the rich man's table; even the dogs would come and lick his sores.

"The poor man died and was carried away by the angels to be with Abraham. The rich man also died and was buried. In Hades, where he was being tormented, he looked up and saw Abraham far away with Lazarus by his side.

"He called out, 'Father Abraham, have mercy on me, and send Lazarus to dip the tip of his finger in water and cool my tongue; for I am in agony in these flames.' But Abraham said, 'Child, remember that during your lifetime you received your good things, and Lazarus in like manner evil things; but now he is comforted here, and you are in agony. Besides all this, between you and us a great chasm has been fixed, so that those who might want to pass from here to you cannot do so, and no one can cross from there to us.'

"He said, 'Then, father, I beg you to send him to my father's house—for I have five brothers—that he may warn them, so that they will not also come into this place of torment.'

"Abraham replied, 'They have Moses and the prophets; they should listen to them.' He said, 'No, father Abraham; but if someone goes to them from the dead, they will repent.' He said to him, 'If they do not listen to Moses and the prophets, neither will they be convinced even if someone rises from the dead.'"

ST. CLARE'S CHURCH, SEPTEMBER 27, 1998

May the words of my mouth and the meditations of my heart be always acceptable in thy sight, O Lord, my strength and my redeemer.

THE PASSAGE WE HAVE just heard is complex and disturbing to say the least. Look how it ends: with the rich man (traditionally called Dives) sent to Hades and his five brothers headed that way. Abraham seems to think that is fine, and so in fact does Jesus. What sense are we to make of this?

It might be helpful to see this story as a series of scenes, or panels or frames, and to look at them one at a time.

In frame one, Dives is rich, enjoying his house and purple linens and feasting. Lazarus is sick, dying of hunger, his sores licked by dogs. This is a picture of human suffering paired with human indifference.

As I imagine it, Dives does not take cruel or sadistic pleasure in the suffering of Lazarus; he is not mean or nasty; he may in fact be rather warm and affectionate towards his friends and family; but to Lazarus he is simply inattentive, blind to what is before him. Lazarus is not real to Dives.

What is implicitly asked of Dives here is not that he give all his money to the poor, nor that he make an extraordinary sacrifice, but only that he discharge the common human obligation to relieve extreme human suffering, and in this case at very little cost to himself.

So Dives represents not just wealth in the face of poverty but a kind of bone-deep indifference to others that is much deeper and more widespread in human nature. This indifference has many sources and takes many forms, but it is surely true that it often arises from wealth, as it does here.

Think what money does: it gives you power over others, and over the circumstances of life as well. If you have it, you think you deserve the advantages, including the power, that it brings you. And you think about it all the time. You worry about your pension fund, or your mortgage, or the market, or what to spend your money on: purple linen and sumptuous feasts. Money draws your attention ineluctably away from its proper objects to false ones.

In this way Dives, whose fault is that he simply does not see Lazarus, manifests the deep pattern of intention and satisfaction, of achievement and possession, on which all of us build much of our lives. Imagine for a minute God as a good parent, to whom we bring back the trophies and achievements of which we are most proud—the promotion or bonus, the new house, the trip to Europe, the book we have written, the Best Teacher prize. Like a good parent, God says:

> Those things are neither good nor bad in themselves. What matters is what they mean to you and to others, what capacities of mind and imagination and feeling they absorb and foster, what relations they enable you to establish with others. Are they founded on love, or on selfishness? The real issue, what I really care about, is what place you give in your life to the recognition of others, to the care of others, to the establishment of loving relations with others—in short, what place you give in your life to the spirit of love.

We are all like Dives, and we all share his disposition not to see, not to feel, all the time.

What exactly is it that Dives does not see and feel? I am reminded here of Dickens's story, *A Christmas Carol*, in which Scrooge's partner Marley is punished after death for the indifference he showed to others when he was alive by being required, as a spirit, to witness human suffering of a sort he could have relieved when he was on earth but did not—say a woman freezing with her child on a doorstep. Now he sees, and feels, and wants to help, but cannot. It is torture.

In frame two Dives is in Hades. This is no surprise to us when we read or hear the story, but we should not slide over the fact that the very idea of Hell is disturbing to us, and in a deep way. What kind of God is it who creates a Hell for those who sin? Here I only mark this question, but I shall soon return to it because I think the parable is partly about it.

Lazarus is in the bosom of Abraham. Why do you suppose Abraham is imagined as taking Lazarus to his bosom in this way? Is it because Lazarus, as a righteous man, adhered to the law, never stole, never coveted what belonged to another, never lied under oath? Surely not. It is because Abraham loves him. He loves him not for his virtue or his merit, but because he is a deeply suffering human being. This is just what Dives could not do, and it is what we are asked to do.

In the third frame Dives asks Abraham to send Lazarus with a drop of water to cool his burning lips. This shows us that Dives has not learned much. He still thinks of Lazarus as a lower being, a kind of lackey to be sent on errands. Dives certainly does not recognize Lazarus' spiritual superiority to him.

Most strikingly, he does not repent. He does not say, "Oh my God, how I have sinned in my indifference to human suffering; have mercy upon me, forgive me." He is still affirming the identity he gave himself through his fixation on linens and feasts and other fine things, and the status they brought him as one who orders servants about. He cannot do otherwise.

A few years ago I spent some time reading through Dante's *Inferno*, and, as I saw it, none of those represented as damned in that poem are shown to repent in any way. They certainly do not like the pain they suffer, but they do not wish they had chosen otherwise. In Dante, Hell is represented as a self-chosen state, and I think the same is true here—though it is chosen by Dives not out of affirmative evil but out of blindness, want of perception, ordinary self-centeredness. Dives is not an especially bad man; he just does not see the human reality that is before him.

This means that Hell is not exclusively a condition of the underworld: it is chosen now. Was Dives in Hell in the first frame, without knowing it? (Without our knowing it? Where then are we?)

In the fourth frame, Abraham says to Dives: "Between you and us a great chasm has been fixed, so that those who might want to pass from here to you cannot do so, and no one can cross from there to us." The point of the story is that this is not a new chasm: it was always there, made by Dives himself when the disparity in power ran the other way. During his life he surely took satisfaction in it. It was a part of his very identity: "I am not like that beggar." Now the tables are turned, and the effect is chilling.

In the fifth frame Dives says, "Send Lazarus to my brothers!" This is a crucial moment, for here Dives does exhibit a concern for others. His request is in fact the beginning of love. This is of course a good thing, but Dives' love is not for Lazarus, whom he still thinks of as a mere messenger, but rather for his brothers, who share his race and class and status.

It is not enough to love your brothers.

Abraham now says to Dives, "They have Moses and the prophets; they should listen to them." They tell them what to do and to be, and the brothers should listen and obey.

Dives responds: "No, father Abraham; but if someone goes to them from the dead, they will repent." His idea is that his brothers do not understand what the law is telling them, but if Lazarus comes back from the dead they will listen and understand.

Abraham's response must give us pause: "If they do not listen to Moses and the prophets, neither will they be convinced even if someone rises from the dead."

This is a profoundly troubling story, particularly in its ending. What sense are we to make of it? It is like a dream, full of disturbing themes and elements; and none of us can be comfortable about where we are in any of the frames or panels.

Let's think of it as one story told to two different audiences, with two rather different meanings.

First let us think of it as a parable told to the Pharisees, the people of prosperity, who have regularly been criticizing Jesus because he keeps company with sinners, poor people, and others beyond the pale of respectability. In the story, the Pharisees are represented by the five brothers: like the brothers, the Pharisees are still alive, still believing that their prosperity is the result of their merit and a sign of God's blessing because they keep his law.

To them Jesus is saying something like this: "This is no way to live. Even your own law tells you to care for someone like Lazarus. I am not talking here as some wild-eyed extremist but simply invoking the law of

Moses, and the words of the prophets too, all of which tell you that you must acknowledge the humanity of the poor and relieve the suffering of the stranger." This is not a command to give everything to the poor, but to discharge the common duties of humanity established by the law. More deeply, it is a command to turn from a life based on possession and achievement, on compliance with the law and other externals, to the reality of the life of the spirit and of the relations we establish with others.

Put even more strongly, Jesus is saying, in effect: "The life you have chosen is, in my terms, no life at all; a kind of death or hell, in which you build a gulf between your fellow man and yourself; when you die, that gulf will become permanent."

We are of course ourselves like the Pharisees, and the message is as stern and chilling to us as it is to them.

But there is another audience for this story, another context, for it all rings very differently when placed against the whole story of Jesus' life. We know from John's Gospel that he did raise another man called Lazarus from the dead, as a sign to his people, to draw their attention to the gift of new life. We also know that Jesus himself came back from the dead, in an effort to reach the hearts and imaginations even of the Pharisees and of us. What does the parable mean against the rest of this story?

I think Jesus is saying something like this. He knows that we have been told over and over again, by the law and by our own experience of life, that we should open our hearts to human poverty and suffering. He knows too that the life of Dives, in which we participate, is a kind of death, and that eternal punishment for choosing it would be fair and just. And he knows that those who, like the brothers, cannot read the lessons of their own hearts, and the lessons of the culture, will probably not be reached by anything, even his own Resurrection.

But Jesus goes on to say that, despite what he knows, he will do it: he will raise that other Lazarus from the dead; he will die for us and return to us, and he will do so with no certainty as to its effect upon us—in fact with only a hope, perhaps a faint one.

What Jesus sees is this: that as Lazarus needed love, so did Dives. In a sense he needed it more, for he thought he needed nothing, and his life of self-satisfaction did not teach him otherwise.

Abraham says to Dives: What about Lazarus?

Jesus says to us: What about Dives?

As Abraham loves Lazarus, Jesus loves those whom it is much harder to love: Dives; the Pharisees; the brothers; us.

On this reading Dives is actually at the center of the story, not Lazarus; Jesus, not Abraham. For Jesus will die for Dives, and for us. We do not deserve it; he knows that his death will not transform every human heart; but he will do it nonetheless. This is his definition of love.

It astonishes the soul.

Amen

This story obviously does not purport to be historically true. It is a myth or parable told by Jesus, mainly to the Pharisees, to whom it is meant to be a warning.

Exactly what kind of truth does it have, if not historical truth? It moves, as myths and parables and fairy tales and science fiction stories often do, by the principle of naturalness and probability. That is: the starting assumption of such a story may be unrealistic, for example that there is a wizard or witch with magical powers or that animals can talk or that on planet Stulton people have eyes in the back of their heads. But given those assumptions, what happens in the story must fit with our sense of what is natural and probable, or people simply will not read or attend to it.

In this parable the main assumption is a vision of life after death as a state in which justice will at last be done: injury redressed and punishment inflicted. It is persuasive and educational because it shows us what is likely to happen, on that assumption, to a person like Dives, and to Lazarus as well.

What is likely to happen to us? Or do we not really believe in a final judgment of this kind?

To return to the question of genre, why does Jesus speak to the Pharisees and his followers, and to us, in a parable, instead of stating simply and directly what he means?

4

Doubting Thomas

This Gospel passage is one of the most famous and most congenial of all: the story of Doubting Thomas. It speaks to everyone who has ever had doubts about his or her faith—including those who have doubts almost all the time, those who almost never have doubts, and those who don't really believe they have faith but just wish they did.

As you read it ask what Thomas felt when he returned to his friends and found that Jesus had been there. What does he want? What do *we* want?

The Gospel of John 20:19–31

When it was evening on that day, the first day of the week, and the doors of the house where the disciples had met were locked for fear of the Jews, Jesus came and stood among them and said, "Peace be with you."

After he said this, he showed them his hands and his side. Then the disciples rejoiced when they saw the Lord. Jesus said to them again, "Peace be with you. As the Father has sent me, so I send you." When he had said this, he breathed on them and said to them, "Receive the Holy Spirit. If you forgive the sins of any, they are forgiven them; if you retain the sins of any, they are retained."

But Thomas (who was called the Twin), one of the twelve, was not with them when Jesus came. So the other disciples told him, "We have seen the Lord." But he said to them, "Unless I see the mark of the nails in his hands, and put my finger in the mark of the nails and my hand in his side, I will not believe."

A week later his disciples were again in the house, and Thomas was with them. Although the doors were shut, Jesus came and stood among them and said, "Peace be with you." Then he said to Thomas, "Put your finger here and see my hands. Reach out your hand and put it in my side. Do not doubt but believe."

Thomas answered him, "My Lord and my God!"

Jesus said to him, "Have you believed because you have seen me? Blessed are those who have not seen and yet have come to believe."

Now Jesus did many other signs in the presence of his disciples, which are not written in this book. But these are written so that you may come to believe that Jesus is the Messiah, the Son of God, and that through believing you may have life in his name.

St. Clare's Church April 7, 2002

May the words of my mouth and the meditations of my heart be always acceptable in thy sight, O Lord, my strength and my redeemer.

The Gospel for today is a favorite passage for many of us, and for obvious reasons.

When the other disciples tell Thomas that Jesus has appeared to them, he frankly states that he does not believe it, and will not believe it unless he sees for himself. In this he speaks for a side of all of us, the side that sometimes, like an imp in the mind, tells us that we do not believe, not any of it; or, in more gentle moments, tells us that we are not sure what we believe, that we are doubters like Thomas. Perhaps this side of us is saying that belief itself is a bad thing, weak and irrational; or perhaps it is saying something very different, which is that our belief is not good enough.

Jesus comes to Thomas, and shows him his wounds, so that Thomas can believe. It seems that Jesus is here accepting Thomas despite his unbelief, accepting his unbelief itself. We are likely to feel that the Gospel is doing the same for us—that it accepts us despite our unbelief—for like Thomas we have not see the Risen Christ either.

So it seems. I think the story is much more complex, and in the end more challenging and disturbing, than that. What happens when we read it slowly, asking what is really happening for these people?

Let us start with the beginning: that Sunday evening, when the disciples were gathered in a room, doors locked for fear of the forces of destruction that had killed Jesus and might kill them. They were hiding, like spies or undercover agents.

What do you think they said to each other? There was nothing positive they could say about the recent events, which were a total and to them unexpected disaster. They were left without the unique and holy person who had given shape and meaning to their lives. They were in real danger, as subsequent events would prove, and they surely felt it. As I imagine it, they huddled together, silently, or maybe with occasional mutterings about how dreadful things were, saying they did not know what on earth to do next. The center had fallen out of the universe and they felt helpless and afraid.

It is to them in this condition that Jesus comes. Why does he do this? Not I think to make a metaphysical or ontological point about his power over physical death, or over other aspects of the physical world. That had been established long ago—think of the raising of Lazarus, for example. Jesus came to meet their present and actual need, as his words show: *"Peace be with you."*

I think what he means by "peace" is something like this: "My peace, which is the opposite of what you now experience: peace as knowledge of who you are, of who I am; peace as the knowledge that you are eternally loved by the God of the universe. You have been full of despair, for you think that all you have is each other, alone in the dark. But you are not alone; you have me too, and you can build your lives on that." Something like this is what he means, but as I imagine it he simply says the words quoted in the Gospel, in the silence: *"Peace be with you."* It is a benediction, like an element in a liturgy.

When Thomas comes back Jesus has gone. He comes back to what was a cold and dark and lonely room, finding it full of hope and joy and meaning, of spiritual warmth and light, and is told that Jesus had been there. He says, in effect, "I will not believe you till I see the wounds myself."

That is what he says, and of course in a way it makes sense. Of course it is easier to believe if you have seen.

But what is Thomas actually feeling? Imagine that we were there, in Thomas's situation: what would we feel? Frustration; disappointment; envy; anger at Jesus and at the disciples; total despair at the center of our being. As I imagine it Thomas says to himself, deep within, "I will never know what they know, never have what they have. I have been left out of the circle of Jesus' love. I am not one of those that matter, and never will be." His heart is broken.

But does he say that? No. And why not? To do so would be to make himself vulnerable to the pity of others, to the very feeling he cannot bear to acknowledge. So he does not say, "My heart is broken, brothers; Jesus loves you and not me"; instead, like any ordinary human being, he takes it out on them—like the child who says, "I did not want that toy anyway," or the employee who says, "You can't fire me. I quit." Thomas says, "I don't believe you and never will."

This of course does not give him happiness, or a sense of belonging, or the restoration of his soul. It is just a lonely, miserable, bitter way of expressing how dreadful he feels—offering him the satisfaction of saying what he sees to be the truth, but indirectly, without admitting it.

Now here is the question: Is it true that Thomas does not believe? I think not. I think he believes, he believes with his whole heart; that is why he is so miserable. He is in fact denying the belief he has, in Jesus and the Resurrection alike. His problem is not disbelief, but denial of belief—because belief is so utterly painful.

A week goes by. A long time in Thomas's life. Once more on Sunday evening, in the same house, the disciples are gathered, and Jesus returns to them. To Thomas he is utterly accepting and loving: he shows him his wounds, and invites Thomas to touch them; in this he shows that he knows not only what Thomas has said to the others but that he knows Thomas himself, knows him in his soul and in his heart. He knows that Thomas has always believed. In the face of this knowledge and love, Thomas does not after all need to touch the wounds, or the body. He simply says: "My Lord and my God!"

The real issue for Thomas is not belief but desolation and Jesus responds to this condition with his presence. So he will respond to ours.

But there is more. The Gospel really does speak to the issue of belief. Jesus makes this explicit when he addresses not Thomas's feelings of desolation but his statement of disbelief: *"Have you believed because you have seen me? Blessed are those who have not seen and yet have come to believe."* John, the Gospel writer, then tells us that this text was written so that those who have not seen, like Thomas after Jesus' first return, may believe.

Belief is not peripheral or unimportant in this passage, but central to it. To Jesus and John alike belief is not a side issue, but the core of Christian life and experience. In this passage we are thus squarely and uncomfortably presented with the question of belief, especially belief in the Resurrection of Christ.

What was the Resurrection really like? I cannot tell you. No one I think can really know. This was an absolutely unique event in the history of the world, and we have no experiences with which to compare it.

What I do know is this: that Jesus utterly transformed the lives of his disciples when he was with them in life, for he was the embodiment of infinite and selfless love. And: that after his Crucifixion he was wholly present to his disciples in that room in Jerusalem, as he was also at Emmaus and by the lakeshore. And: that he is present today, in our lives, especially in the Eucharist we are about to share. This is not merely a remembrance of something that happened two thousand years ago, nor a reenacted sacrifice, but an affirmation of the immediate presence of Christ here, now, in this room.

When Jesus returns to the disciples, both times, his presence restores them, heals them, makes them whole once more. It brings *them* back to life too, individually and as a community. This is what enables Thomas to affirm the faith he has been denying: "My Lord and My God!"

But there is another element to what Jesus offers. When he first returns to his disciples, after he has said, *"Peace be with you,"* he adds something else: *"As the Father has sent me, so I send you."* He sends them on a mission. The peace he grants is thus not a peace of repose or quiet or satisfaction or ease, but a kind of inner knowledge that will enable them to act in the dangerous world they fear. This "peace" implies a whole way of life, full of risk and uncertainty; it is not a gratification of self but a loss of self in service.

Jesus then breathes the Holy Spirit upon his disciples as a way of equipping them for the life to which he sends them: the building of his Church, which will require them to suffer hunger, prison, stoning, martyrdom, crucifixion upside down, and all the other pains, mortifications, and agonies it entails. He is saying in effect: "I send you to a life founded on truth and love. It will be costly to you, painful to you, as my life has been to me." When the Father sent Jesus it was to his Crucifixion, and Jesus says: *"As the Father has sent me, so I send you."*

The disciples may have been filled at first with simple joy and gladness at his return; but not long after they must have begun to be afraid again, not of the people John calls the Jews, but of what the life on which they are here launched will mean for them, of the truth and reality they will have to face. Whatever comes will not be easy, and it may be horrific.

We are of course included in Jesus' commission; he is sending us too into the world. Belief means recognizing that fact. The life to which he sends us may not end in crucifixion, though that could happen. What we are told is to live, joyfully, a life that could bring us to that end, or one similarly agonizing, if the service of Christ requires it. This will be hard, maybe harder than we can bear. It will mean confronting the truth about ourselves, including our failures of belief and perception alike, and living with the recognition of our weakness and sin.

This may be why, like Thomas, we find ourselves sometimes denying our own belief and knowledge and experience, our awareness of the presence of Christ in the world: not out of desolation and anger, like Thomas, but out of something equally human, though less worthy: fear of what it may mean. This is why Jesus says to us and to others so often: "Be not afraid"; "Don't be afraid"; "Fear not"; "Peace be unto you."

We don't know for sure what happened next in Thomas's life, but there is a tradition that he traveled alone to India, southern India, where he established the church that continues there to this day. Once Thomas knew that Jesus was with him, he was inspired to great and dangerous and solitary action.

I like to think that as Thomas sailed across the Arabian Sea to India, his heart sang within him. He was scared, but not afraid, for he was living out of the truth, the truth of Jesus' love for him. May our hearts also sing as we take the truth of God's love, God's love of truth, as the basis for our own lives, our own costly and dangerous action, in the world.

Amen

One issue it is impossible for a twenty-first century reader not to notice, in this passage and in the Gospels more generally—especially the Gospel of John—is the role of the people here called "the Jews" and the sorts of feelings that the reader seems to be invited to have towards them. Is this way of talking and thinking the beginning of Christian anti-Semitism?

Let us think of this question at two moments in time: the moment of Jesus' death and Resurrection and the moment, maybe sixty years later, when the Gospel was composed. Let us think, that is, first of the story itself and then of the way it is told.

It is clear to start with that both Jesus and all of his disciples and apostles were Jews, that is, persons raised in the traditions of the people of Israel, including the law of the Hebrew Bible. If there was an ethnic difference between Jews and others, Jesus and his followers were ethnically Jewish as well. So they cannot be experiencing an ethnic animosity towards Jewish people of the kind that found its hideous expression in Hitler's mass murders in the twentieth century. Nor can they be expressing a rejection of the religion of Israel, for Jesus thought he was fulfilling that religion, in which he was raised, not replacing it with some new religion called Christianity.

To what then were Jesus and his friends opposed? It seems that it was a particular structure of power, based upon the Temple establishment and cooperating with the Roman Empire. It is relevant that the term translated as "Jews," namely the Greek word *Ioudaioi*, also means Judeans, that is, people from the territory of what had been the southern kingdom and especially from its capital, Jerusalem. It was the Judeans who ruled over the rest of what we would now call Israel, and did so in cooperation with the Roman Empire.

On the other hand, *Ioudaios* is sometimes used to mark a person of orthodox Jewish belief, as opposed to other worshippers of Yahweh, like the Samaritans. Jesus himself accepts his own description as a *Ioudaios* in his conversation with the Samaritan woman at the well, even though he is of course from the north (John 4:9–22). So *Ioudaios* does mean "Jew" where a line is being drawn between orthodox Yahwists and others; but where a line is being drawn among the orthodox Yahwists, between those who support the Temple establishment and its connection with Rome, and those who do not, it means "Judean." In the passage from John it is pretty clear that the people of whom the apostles are afraid are not "the Jews" in any ethnic or religious sense, but supporters of the Judean power structure.

By the time John writes the Gospel, the original situation has become complicated. The Christian community to which, and out of which, John is writing now includes gentiles and, perhaps partly for this reason, there is tension between this community and the Jewish diaspora. This is not a tension between the Temple establishment and the rest of the Jewish world, for the Temple has been destroyed. Judaism now exists mainly in the form of independent communities of worship, spread throughout the Mediterranean basin and the Middle East. Conflict had apparently developed over time between traditional Jewish congregations and those who were starting to call themselves Christian, perhaps because they were competing for members of the same population.

I think we cannot know in detail what the tension consisted of, but it was almost certainly not ethnic, nor was it an opposition between two wholly different religious systems. It was really a struggle internal to a religious community that had included both elements but resulted in their separation. The critical issues may have had to do with the control of buildings and property claimed by both groups, both groups in some sense being Jewish—one believing that the Messiah had come, the other believing that he had not. It was no doubt exacerbated by the fact that what we call Christianity was a proselytizing religion, as more traditional Judaism probably was not. There is some evidence in John's Gospel that the people of his community were excluded from the synagogues to which they had formerly belonged (John 9:22). It seems that there was animosity on both sides of the emerging divide.

None of this is of course to deny that the language used here, placed in different contexts over centuries and millennia, has been used to foster anti-Semitism, for it surely has. Nor is it to deny that the Christian Church has in various ways and times had strong anti-Semitic strains, for that is also surely true. It is only to say that it is too easy to read the Gospel of John, especially in translation, as though it had—indeed as though Jesus and his followers had—an anti-Semitic animus of a kind that foreshadowed the anti-Semitism of recent centuries.

5

Walking on Water

One of Jesus' most famous miracles was walking on water, an action we find described both in Matthew (Matthew 14:22–33) and in Mark, the version that appears below. As both writers tell the story, the event takes place during the night after the miracle of the loaves and fishes, in which Jesus fed five thousand people with just a few loaves of bread and a couple of fish.

Why does Jesus walk on the water? What does this enable him to achieve? Maybe he is demonstrating extraordinary power: What kind of power is this, to whom is he demonstrating it, and what is its point?

Where are we in this story?

> *The Gospel of Mark 6:45–52*
>
> Immediately he made his disciples get into the boat and go on ahead to the other side, to Bethsaida, while he dismissed the crowd. After saying farewell to them, he went up on the mountain to pray.
>
> When evening came, the boat was out on the sea, and he was alone on the land. When he saw that they were straining at the oars against an adverse wind, he came towards them early in the morning, walking on the sea. He intended to pass them by. But when they saw him walking on the sea, they thought it was a ghost and cried out; for they all saw him and were terrified.

But immediately he spoke to them and said, "Take heart, it is I; do not be afraid." Then he got into the boat with them and the wind ceased. And they were utterly astounded, for they did not understand about the loaves, but their hearts were hardened.

St. Andrew's Church, July 27, 2003

May the words of my mouth and the meditations of my heart be always acceptable in thy sight, O Lord, my strength and my redeemer.

TODAY WE HEARD THE famous story about Jesus walking on water. As you may know, there is a place on the Sea of Galilee where an imaginative entrepreneur has built a concrete platform just an inch or two below the surface of the water; for a fee you can walk out on this subsurface pier and have your photo taken, walking on the water, serenely suspended as it were upon its surface. Or you may remember seeing Peter Sellers doing something similar in the movie *Being There*, a saintly madman walking peacefully out on the still surface of a lake. But this is not what Jesus was doing: there was no concrete pier beneath the surface, and he was not slowly stepping onto a smooth lake, but making his way through violent waves, in the middle of a windy night. This is a totally different image: weird, wild, otherworldly. It is about Jesus' identity and power.

In some ways the story makes perfect sense. Jesus has just fed the five thousand. He is no doubt exhausted by this public exercise of his powers, and perhaps a bit afraid too. He needs to be alone, to pray to his Father, and he sends the disciples on ahead, saying that he will join them later. But in fact he seems to have a bit of a conflict about rejoining them, for Mark tells us that when he is walking on the sea he wants to pass right by. Perhaps he does not want to face the responsibility they represent.

As for the disciples, they have been separated from Jesus by his command, sent away on the sea. He says he will follow them, but they may well wonder whether he will really do that, and if so how, and when. What if he does not? As I imagine them, they are anxious and upset, worried about what will happen next, afraid—perhaps more afraid than they know—as they find themselves laboring at their oars against a strong wind.

No wonder, then, that they are frightened and astounded by the image of Jesus walking through the stormy waves, in the dark. He must indeed have seemed like a ghost, as Mark says, a ghost confirming their fear that Jesus had died and telling them that the separation they were experiencing was forever. But Jesus comes to them, reassuring them that it is indeed he, that he is not dead, that what they are seeing is not a spirit or ghost. The waves are calmed.

The disciples are astounded; but Mark is unsympathetic with them and tells us that the reason they are astounded is that, as usual, they did not understand something, in this case the miracle of the loaves. If they had understood that, he implies, they would not have been surprised to see Jesus walking over the waves on a windy night. Instead their hearts were hardened.

All this presents an unavoidable question, which Mark suggests but does not answer: What exactly is it that the disciples do not understand, and that we, as readers of the Gospel, in Mark's time or our own, are supposed to understand?

I think what Mark wants us to see is this: that Jesus is not just a wonderful man, wise and loving, a true prophet, but is somehow connected to the force and power that created the whole world and everything in it. To Jesus the five loaves of bread are the material for feeding five thousand people; for Jesus the stormy seas subside; for him it is possible to pass through a storm on the lake unharmed, walking through the tumultuous waves. This is the same force and power that separated the waters of the Red Sea for the children of Israel; the power at which the hills and mountains skip like rams and young sheep in Psalm 114; the power that in the same psalm made water spring from a rock; and the power that swept Elijah up in a whirlwind (2 Kings 2:11).

Mark does not have our doctrinal language of the Trinity—in which Jesus is the Son of God, "begotten, not made"—with which to tell us who Jesus is. But I think that his lack of conceptual understanding does not much matter to Mark, for he is just not very interested in doctrine. His task in this Gospel is to set forth directly and simply the way Jesus revealed himself in his acts and speeches, not to explain it theologically. His text is rapid, urgent, tracing out Jesus' career as if he were a flaming light that transforms everything it touches. This Jesus is as little apprehensible by our words and minds as are the prayers that he utters to his Father on the mountain, of which we hear nothing. In Mark there is always a background of mystery against which the revelation occurs, and so it is here.

I think the real reason the disciples do not understand who Jesus is and what he has done is that they do not really want to acknowledge what that would mean, and neither do we. It is fine for Jesus to be a wise and good man, purely loving, purely self-sacrificing, purely peaceful; it is all right even for him to be able to heal the sick and feed the hungry, and to do other good deeds.

But that he should have the power to shoot lightning from his fingertips, or make the mountains dance and the rivers dry up, or to walk through the windy night across the Sea of Galilee is highly uncomfortable, to say the least, to them and to us. As Mark sees it, the presence of Jesus on earth is like the presence of the God of Israel on Mount Sinai, utterly transforming everything, including the natural world. Perhaps he is saying, with the psalmist, "Tremble thou earth at the presence of the Lord" (Psalm 114:7). No wonder the disciples, and we, do not want to recognize what we are being told.

Even if we do recognize his power, how are we to make sense of it? How are we to put together the two central facts about Jesus revealed here, his love and his power? His life is not *about* his power, but he has it; it is crucial that he has it, and that we know that he has it, and for a paradoxical reason—for the ways in which he does *not* use it. He does not use his power against others, not ever, not even at the most crucial point in his life, his Crucifixion. He uses it to heal, to feed, to cure—never to compel, or force, or overcome.

His power is in fact essential to the meaning of the Crucifixion, for the fact of his power makes clear that Jesus is voluntarily submitting to the force of human evil, not being overcome by it. This is not a case in which a good man is caught and overpowered and killed by bad ones. At his Crucifixion Jesus refuses to exercise one kind of godly power, power over the physical world, in order to demonstrate the reality and validity and force of another kind of power, also godly, that of love and truth. For Jesus changed the world infinitely more deeply, more lovingly, and more powerfully, by dying on the cross than he would have done had he called upon legions of angels to rescue him.

All this speaks directly to us, for our culture has a very different sense of the nature and value of power. It is full of voices telling us that power is a good thing; that the purpose of life is to acquire it and exercise it to get what you want in the world. Power—perhaps mainly in the form of money, but not only that—is essential to the satisfactions we seek in life, to what our culture holds out as human fulfillment.

We all in fact have power: not infinite power of course, but real power: personal, social, economic, cultural power. We can make things happen in the world, in our family, in our church, with our friends. How are we to use this power? If we take Jesus seriously we are not to use it to gratify ourselves, not to overcome others, not to try to reduce them to our will, not to manipulate, but only to heal, to cure, to comfort, to help: to recognize the needs and feelings of others and to respond to them lovingly.

The Christian image of life here, as always, is radical and total in its demand upon us. It is deeply upsetting, for it calls for a wholly different way of imagining ourselves and others and our life together, based not upon power and self, but upon selflessness and love.

Can we achieve that life? Of course not perfectly. Such are the limitations of our nature. But we can aim at it, seek it, struggle for it. And by walking through the waves on a windy night Jesus shows us, and his disciples, something crucial about the life to which he calls us: that it is based not on weakness, incapacity, timidity, and cowardice, but the opposite of these things: courage, strength, ability, and vast power—power that is to be used only in the service of others, not ourselves.

He shows us something else as well: that even if we do not understand, even if our hearts are hardened, he will still come to us as we labor at our oars on a stormy night, and say, *"Take heart; it is I; do not be afraid."*

Amen

There is a wonderful moment in this story, when we are told that Jesus went up to the mountain to pray to his Father. Why did he go up the mountain? Could he not have prayed perfectly easily on a rooftop in a town, or in a private room, or even by the side of the road?

What was his prayer? Was it expressed in words, and if so what were they? Indeed if it did take the form of words, why does he not tell us what the words were so that we can use them too? If the prayer was not in words, what was it?

Was the prayer a conversation of some sort? Can our prayer be like that?

By stimulating such questions about Jesus' prayer, the passage invites us to think about our own prayer too, about prayer itself. Do we pray in words? In what words? Do we pray wordlessly?

What is our prayer? What should it be?

I think this line of questions about prayer is surprisingly connected to the fact that this story is partly about power. Mainly the power is Jesus' power, of course, but there is also another kind of power here, exemplified especially by Mark, which is power not over the sea but over oneself: the power to tell the truth. For that is what Mark is doing here: telling us a truth about the nature of Jesus that the disciples could not quite grasp. For Mark the story of Jesus walking on water is not a metaphor, not a fantasy, but the simplest and amazing truth, the direct revelation of divine power, and he exercises the real power of telling it as it is.

We too have power to tell the truth, and to call upon ourselves and others to live out of the truth. Think how often we have failed in this: failed to stand up against a bigoted remark, or for a humiliated person, or against lies and cruelty and force; failed to protect a child, or an ill or aged person; failed to state the truth as we see it. Every such failure is the failure to exercise a power that we have and a part of what allows the systems of brutality that mar our world to continue in force.

Mark knows this. His effort is to tell the truth. This requires courage in him, as it does in us. The truth he states here is that Jesus is not merely a very good man and ethical teacher, not even a person of superhuman love, but a person with access to divine power, the power that created and still shapes the world.

Can we say that? Have we the knowledge and courage to say that the Christ in whom we believe was God as well as man, that he walked through the storm on the water? That he fed the five thousand? That he brought Jairus' daughter back to life? That he himself rose from the dead?

To say these things may make us afraid, socially and intellectually afraid. It is embarrassing to believe such things, and the truth of them is fearful. They are like this scene on the Sea of Galilee, wild and weird. Can we tell that truth? Mark did, and shows us how to do it, and calls upon us to do likewise. But we are afraid.

Is this the point at which we should go up a mountain alone to pray?

6

The Good Samaritan

This is another classic parable, deep in our culture. It is the subject of a wonderful etching by Rembrandt, and of paintings by other artists as well. The phrase "good Samaritan" is a part of ordinary conversational English. But what does this story mean?

Here it is important to understand that the Samaritans, despised by the Judeans, were also worshippers of Yahweh. In fact, in their view they adhered to the original religious tenets of Judaism, especially the central practice of sacrifice in the high places (as in fact they still do). They rejected the Judean requirement of sacrifice and worship in the Temple in Jerusalem, and with it the whole economic and political hierarchy of the Judeans, who to them were relative upstarts.

But power was in the hands of the Judeans, who had contempt for the Samaritans and regarded them as unclean. For a Judean to touch a Samaritan, or a corpse, would have been a pollution, requiring ritual cleansing. This may help explain why the two men—the priest (namely, a priest of the Temple) and the Levite (a different kind of priest)—pass by the unknown injured man, who might have been dead.

The Gospel of Luke 10:25-37

Just then a lawyer stood up to test Jesus. "Teacher," he said, "what must I do to inherit eternal life?" He said to him, "What is written in the law? What do you read there?" He answered, "You shall love the Lord your God with all your heart, and with all your soul, and with all your strength, and with all your mind; and your neighbor as yourself." And he said to him, "You have given the right answer; do this, and you will live."

But wanting to justify himself, he asked Jesus, "And who is my neighbor?"

Jesus replied, "A man was going down from Jerusalem to Jericho, and fell into the hands of robbers, who stripped him, beat him, and went away, leaving him half dead. Now by chance a priest was going down that road; and when he saw him, he passed by on the other side. So likewise a Levite, when he came to the place and saw him, passed by on the other side.

"But a Samaritan while traveling came near him; and when he saw him, he was moved with pity. He went to him and bandaged his wounds, having poured oil and wine on them. Then he put him on his own animal, brought him to an inn, and took care of him. The next day he took out two denarii, gave them to the innkeeper, and said, 'Take care of him; and when I come back, I will repay you whatever more you spend.'

"Which of these three, do you think, was a neighbor to the man who fell into the hands of the robbers?" He said, "The one who showed him mercy." Jesus said to him, "Go and do likewise."

The Church of the Mediator, July 11, 2002

May the words of my mouth and the meditations of my heart be always acceptable in thy sight, O Lord, my strength and my redeemer.

WE HAVE JUST HEARD one of the most famous passages in the New Testament, the parable of the Good Samaritan. For many of us this narrative has been a part of life since childhood: the story of the man beaten by robbers, left for dead by the highway, disdainfully ignored by the passers by, then cared for wonderfully by the Good Samaritan. Its message is in a sense a simple one: be like the Samaritan. But the way it is developed is not so simple.

To start with, Jesus does not tell this story to the air, or to us; he tells it to the lawyer who, wishing to tempt or test him, asks him, "What must I do to inherit eternal life?" In the other places in the Gospels where we hear a similar question posed, for example by "the rich young man" (e.g., in Luke 18:18–30), Jesus answers by reciting several of the ten commandments, or by telling his questioner the two most important commandments, to love God and your neighbor.

But this time Jesus responds to the lawyer's question with a question: *"What is written in the law?"* Now it is not Jesus but the lawyer who quotes the two great commandments: "You shall love the Lord your God with all your heart, and with all your soul, and with all your strength, and with all your mind; and your neighbor as yourself."

This man is telling Jesus, that is, just what Jesus normally tells the others. Jesus approves, wholeheartedly, saying, *"You have given the right answer; do this, and you will live."*

This could be the end of the story. The lawyer is told he has got it right and he could have walked away satisfied. But he just can't help asking another question, a lawyer's question: "Who is my neighbor?" As a lawyer myself I have to say that this is still how lawyers think: "Define your terms." Here, as often, the point of the lawyer's question is to define the extent of an obligation: Whom am I to love? And, by implication, How much? What, that is, are the limits on my obligation?

This is the point at which Jesus tells him the parable of the Good Samaritan. It is a way of answering the lawyer's question, and the answer is, "There is no limit." The man injured by the road is your neighbor, whoever he is: Jew or Gentile, Samaritan or priest; all suffering people are your neighbors; and your task in loving them is to make their sufferings wholly your own, as the Samaritan did.

For the Samaritan does not simply call for an ambulance or take the man to the emergency room or give him twenty dollars. He takes him to the inn, and dresses his wounds with his own hands; he then assumes responsibility for his bill, including charges that will accrue in the future. He does not just help the injured man, he makes him his own, as if he were a member of his household. There is no line between him and the man he is helping: he treats him as a child or brother. There is no limit on his love.

To see how remarkable this is, just imagine how you or I might behave if we came upon a sick or injured person, say in an alley or doorway. We might well pass by, as the two priests did; if we did anything at all we might call for help, and think our job done, or maybe lend or give a little money; but, like the lawyer, at every stage we would be asking where the limit is, where the line should be drawn. We live in a world in which drawing appropriate boundaries is thought to be essential to social and psychological health. But for the Samaritan there is no limit, no line, no boundary. He says to the innkeeper, in effect, "Treat him as you would treat me."

Remember the question that started this off: "What must I do to inherit eternal life?" Jesus tells the lawyer, and us, in essence, "Do what the Samaritan did." By this I do not think he means that if you do this painful and difficult thing called "helping someone" you will get something else, somewhere else, called "eternal life" as a reward, but something far deeper and more revolutionary: this—what the Samaritan does and is—*is* eternal life. This is what I mean by living, Jesus is telling us: loving all, and loving all the way. *"Do this, and you will live."*

For you and me all this is most uncomfortable, for which of us meets this standard? Which of us makes everyone his or her neighbor, and then makes their suffering his or her own? I constantly hear, and I imagine you do too, the voice of the lawyer within, asking, "Who is my neighbor? How much do I have to do for him?" In all fairness there *has* to be a limit somewhere, I say; if I give everything away I shall be homeless too and so will my children and spouse; I will not be able to discharge my other responsibilities; and anyway there are far too many injured and suffering people in the world for me to help all of them in this way, to make them all my own. It is not fair or right to ask this of me. There just has to be a limit—so I join the lawyer in asking Jesus to tell me what the limit is.

It does make sense to say that there has to be a limit on your giving of yourself, or there will be no self left. Some people who care for others—say the parents of a deeply damaged child—know that to be so, for their lives are utterly devoured by what they do. There is nothing left. Some people, perhaps in this parish, reach and even exceed the limit. But most of us do not; we do not in fact come close. I know I do not.

One thing I imagine Jesus saying to me, then, when I start to talk about limits and boundaries, is something like this: "Are you at your limit? Are you even close? Are you within ten miles? When you do get to the limit, then you can speak to me of such things; but not now, not yet."

If he went on to explain, Jesus might say something like this:

When you ask these questions about limits—"Who is my neighbor? How much should I love him?"—you are making a basic mistake. In one sense you "know" what you need to know, for, like the lawyer, you can repeat the language about loving God and your neighbor and do so perfectly. But the fact that you ask this question shows that you really do not know what it means. You do not understand the fundamental character of the call I am making to you. Like the lawyer, you are trying to control the nature of your commitment intellectually, even strategically, and that is not the nature of the love to which I call you.

You are like a man who asks a woman to marry him, declaring undying love and joy; when she says, "Oh, yes!" he proposes that they now draft a contract regulating all the details of their relationship and determining what happens if it comes to an end. This is not the way to love.

The love of which Jesus speaks is not a program or a decision or a strategy or an obligation, but a felt commitment of the whole being—like the love you feel for your child or spouse. It is real love: a movement of the whole heart, made in faith and hope and trust; a movement that is hobbled and crippled by any attempt to rationalize it, to structure it, to control it. When two young people are in love they commit themselves to each other in love and pleasure. They do not spend their time anticipating difficulties or making contracts, and if they did it would interfere with what they should be doing, which is bonding in joy.

Jesus is holding out the possibility that our love of God and our neighbor could be like that, total and life-giving. To live out of this kind of love, as the Samaritan did, would be to live not out of a sense of duty, to be carefully measured and defined, but out of an essential aspect of oneself, in joy.

This gets us back to the question of limits: this time not the limits the lawyer wants to set on the obligation, as a matter of justice, but the limits of our actual nature. Maybe we can see and imagine this kind of love, but we also know that we can attain it, if at all, only from time to time, in moments and fragments. We cannot make it the sole principle of our lives. We just cannot.

This is true, but it is not a ground for despair or giving up on Jesus or ourselves or the world. It suggests in fact another way of reading and connecting with the parable Jesus tells. We cannot have the kind of perfect love the Samaritan represents, but Jesus can, as the rest of his life will show.

Jesus is telling us, I think, something like this: "The command to love with your whole heart, to love another as yourself, is in a sense impossible. But you do not have to face this impossibility alone. You have me, and my love, which has no limit. I make all humanity's suffering my own, including yours. You may not be able to love as the Samaritan does, but I can and do."

We are in this story, then—and so is the lawyer—not only as the one who is asked to love as the Samaritan loves, and cannot do it, but as the injured and beaten person by the roadway, as the one who is loved. This love is the promise of the Gospel and of the Church; and it is this love—experienced here in this church, in the Eucharist, in our families—that makes our lives possible, broken and failed as they are in so many ways; it is what we mean by redemption. It makes possible, too, what would otherwise be unimaginable, our own hope of glimpsing eternal life in our daily life.

Amen

In this story there is something we are not told, something that would have been crucial to any of the actors within it, and to its original audience as well, namely, the social status of the injured man. He could have been a Jew, maybe even a Temple priest or a Levite, or himself a Samaritan or a member of some other despised group. When Jesus fails to tell us the social identity of the helpless man, he is saying that it should not have mattered at all.

A helpful comparison might be race in America: if you are introduced to a person you almost always know his or her race, and, if you do not, this very fact is likely to make you feel uncomfortable. For in our world everyone has a race. It is mandatory. A friend of my daughter was of mixed race of a kind that was difficult for people to identify and part of her experience was having people come up to her and ask the incredibly rude question, "What are you?" That they asked such a question is itself a sign of the degree of anxiety they felt: they simply had to know what race they should assign to her; if they could not figure it out, they would ask.

Similarly in the world in which Jesus is telling this story, it would be crucial for you to know the socially determined identity of anyone you met. Your attitude towards him and what he did would be deeply shaped by whether he was a Jew, or a Roman, or a Samaritan. This was in some ways a caste society.

So is ours.

What does this fact mean for us? Think of this, for example: If we found ourselves in a situation like that of the two priests in the story, coming upon someone in the street who was injured or unwell, would our decision to help or pass by be affected by the race of the suffering person? By his or her apparent wealth or poverty, or class status? If so, what do we do with that fact about ourselves?

7

The Narrow Door

The passage from Luke that follows below presents us with questions we would much rather not have to face: Who will be saved? Who will not? Why is *anyone* not to be saved? In fact, how can we possibly put the whole idea of condemnation together with our image of an infinitely loving God?

As Jesus makes clear, these are real questions even for the disciples themselves, whom he warns not to rely upon the fact that they have been his friends and associates.

Finally, and not least: How can we know into which class we shall fall, the saved or the unsaved?

The Gospel of Luke 13:22–30

Jesus went through one town and village after another, teaching as he made his way to Jerusalem. Someone asked him, "Lord, will only a few be saved?"

He said to them, "Strive to enter through the narrow door; for many, I tell you, will try to enter and will not be able. When once the owner of the house has got up and shut the door, and you begin to stand outside and to knock at the door, saying, 'Lord, open to us,' then in reply he will say to you, 'I do not know where you come from.' Then you will begin to say, 'We ate and drank with you, and you taught in our streets.' But he will say, 'I do not know where you come from; go away from me, all you evildoers!'

"There will be weeping and gnashing of teeth when you see Abraham and Isaac and Jacob and all the prophets in the kingdom of God, and you yourselves thrown out. Then people will come from east and west, from north and south, and will eat in the kingdom of God. Indeed, some are last who will be first, and some are first who will be last."

The Church of the Mediator, August 22, 2004

May the words of my mouth and the meditations of my heart be always acceptable in thy sight, O Lord, my strength and my redeemer.

THE READINGS FROM SCRIPTURE today are formidable, to say the least. In Isaiah we hear of the impending destruction of those who have made "a covenant with death" (Isaiah 28:15). In the letter to the Hebrews we are warned, "Our God is a consuming fire" (Hebrews 12:29). And in Luke's Gospel Jesus tells us that there will be many who seek to enter the kingdom, but who will not be able to do so, for the door is a narrow one. Having closed the door, the Master will deny entrance to those outside. You will look upon Abraham and Isaac and Jacob feasting in the kingdom of God, Jesus tells his listeners, but you yourselves will be thrust out.

This image of exclusion from God's company at the feast is especially hard for us in our culture, for we do not talk much about such things. Sin and its consequences, the reality of hell, and the judgment of God are not regular topics in our thought. Yet the God we see in action in both the Old Testament and the New Testament is capable of great and violent destruction. This passage is of course not the only one in which Jesus says such things as, "The first shall be last and the last shall be first." His utterances in the Gospels in fact have a great deal in them about exclusion, about rejection, about not being saved, and so on.

What are we to do, then, with a passage like this one?

One starting point, as always, is to think about what Jesus says, not in the abstract but with attention to the context in which it occurs. Here that context is a question from a man who asks him, "Lord, will only a few be saved?" There are many possible ways to understand this questioner and his question. Maybe he is fearful for his own future, maybe he is concerned for the suffering of others; but my own sense is that he is certain that he will be saved and wants to know exactly how exclusive this club he is joining will be. Perhaps he even takes pleasure at the prospect of looking out the window at all those in the street who, being less virtuous, or less well connected, do not make it in.

Something like this might explain why Jesus is angry at him, because he is presumptuous. And Jesus *is* angry: he takes pains to tell his questioner that he cannot possibly know whether he will be admitted or excluded, and that if he is excluded, it will do him no good to say that he has eaten and drunk with Jesus. "Don't count on it, friend," is what Jesus is saying. This is all a serious warning to the smug.

The obvious problem for us is that we are smug too. I remember reading some years ago the results of a survey showing that the overwhelming majority of people in this country—over 90 percent—believe in God; that nearly all of us believe in heaven; that very few of us believe in hell; and that almost no one thinks they are in any danger of going there. We seem to enjoy a sublime confidence that we are on the right track. Everything will work out for us.

The Gospel story in fact demonstrates that something like this is in fact true of us, by the reaction it creates in us as readers. It does this in a surprising but disturbingly effective way. As we hear Luke's story, we are likely to find ourselves thinking that the person questioning Jesus is extremely unattractive, as myself did a few moments ago. He seems certain that he is to be saved, and does not want to have to share his elect status too widely, for that would depreciate it. He may actually enjoy the sense of his superiority to those who will be sent elsewhere. He is self-righteous and sure that God is on his side; he may remind us of people like him, either in our daily lives or on the national scene, whom we really dislike. We read this story knowing we are not like him, and glad of it.

But notice what has happened to us. The instant we feel superior to the questioner—this man we want to call a self-righteous prig—we are being in an essential way just like him. Our effort to differentiate ourselves from the man to whom we feel so superior, is really no better than his effort to differentiate himself from those who will not be saved. In essentials it is exactly the same, because we feel, whether consciously or not, that this man will not be saved, a matter as to which we cannot possibly have certain knowledge. This means that we are ourselves right in the middle of the story—that we ourselves *are* the questioner—and that Jesus' anger is directed at us, as well as him. It is *our* mistaken self-assurance that Jesus is addressing here. He is telling us that we may not be saved after all. Our souls are at risk.

The discovery of our misplaced sense of superiority to the one who asks the question makes real and vivid for us in a new way what Jesus says about salvation—that some will be saved and some not—and it is not a comfortable thought. When we recognize that we may not be saved, we may protest, "What kind of God is it who will shut the door on us, or consume us with fire? I thought our God was a God of love and forgiveness; why would he not save anyone who wanted to be saved? Would he really send me to hell for ever and ever because of my sins? What can the Bible mean when it talks about him in such a way?"

It may help to think about this issue not in terms of being eternally saved or damned, of heaven and hell, but in terms of ordinary human experience. We can begin with this. It is an undeniable fact of human life that we do much to form our own souls and characters as we live, day by day; and we do this for good and for bad. If we make it our habit to think of ourselves always first, we become increasingly selfish and competitive; if we think of others first, with care and love, without envy or competition, we become increasingly loving and caring. This is a fact of our moral lives.

We also know, when we look around us, that there are people whose lives seem to us deep, and rich, and serene, who somehow have real access to wisdom and humility; but others whose lives seem empty or superficial, caught up in activities that do not bring life or love to themselves or to other people. We know that sometimes we see one set of possibilities realized in ourselves, sometimes the other.

It matters a lot, then, what habits we practice, and especially how we stand in relation to the sufferings and joys of others, not so much because we are going to be punished sometime for being bad, but because this shapes who we actually are. When we come to the end of life—which for any of us may be at any moment, as Jesus often reminds us—we will each be faced with an immutable fact: this is what is I have made of myself, of my life, and it cannot be changed. Even God cannot change it.

As the passage from Isaiah suggests, it is actually possible for us as free moral actors to make a covenant with death. Some people do that.

Maybe we do that, without knowing it. As Jesus tells us in this story, we cannot really know for sure the meaning of what we do and are.

I think the main concern of this passage is accordingly not so much with the afterlife, with exclusion and inclusion, as with how we should lead our lives under the conditions of deep uncertainty that we necessarily face. Jesus is telling us where our attention should be focused: not on whether some other person has made a covenant with death, but on whether we ourselves have done so. We should think of the narrow door to the kingdom, and whether we shall be able to enter by it, not whether someone else will be able to do so. For whenever we focus on questions of comparative virtue, or competition for excellence or for salvation, or the faults of other people, however prominent and irritating those faults may be, we are misdirecting our attention, just as Jesus' questioner was doing. Our attention should be not on others, their faults and their fate, but on the quality of our own spiritual lives, including our own sinfulness and selfishness and competitiveness and emptiness, and our smug self-righteousness too.

"But," you may ask, "even if we do try to focus our attention this way, can we be sure that we will make ourselves worthy of the narrow gate?" The answer is plain and painful: if we have only ourselves to rely on, the answer will always be no. Our own unaided efforts, which are always flawed, will never be enough. This is what original sin means. It is an essential ingredient of our nature and our situation.

But in the Gospel we are promised something else, something that Jesus in his anger at our smugness does not mention, though it is the true message of his whole life: that if we turn with open hearts to the principle of love in the universe, as it is active in ourselves and other people, our lives will be transformed, utterly transformed. We will not become perfect, for we are always flawed; but we will be different. This is not a promise of eternal life sometime after we die, but a promise of a change of life now, in the world—a promise of participation now in the life that is always and is eternal, the life of equality and mutuality and love.

We each know some people who have undergone this kind of change: it shows in their eyes and smile, in their strength and serenity, in their wisdom and gentleness. If we turn our hearts in the direction they have turned theirs, and open them to what we find there, we can in our own ways be transformed too. Of course we cannot do it perfectly; we shall continue to fail; but if we ask for forgiveness in a genuine way, and ourselves seek to forgive others, we shall be forgiven over and over.

Jesus is telling us to give our attention to what love always looks to: the reality and goodness of other people, and our relation with them as equal beings, equal sinners, equal children of God.

The Gospel promises us a covenant, a new covenant, into which we can enter if we choose; if we do, we will be so busy being alive, in each other's presence and the presence of God, that we will forget about who is saved and who is not, and what happens to the others. We will forget even about what happens to us.

This is the covenant of life our God offers us, not the covenant of death of which Isaiah spoke. In the sacrament of the Eucharist in which we are about to engage we shall have an opportunity to affirm that covenant and the transformation it promises us.

Amen

I asked at the beginning of the sermon whether God really will punish people eternally for their sins, and, if so, how this could possibly be consistent with his essential lovingness, his constant readiness to forgive. The answer suggested is that one kind of condemnation is indeed a realistic possibility, namely, the condemnation that is self-inflicted: our own transformation of ourselves into unloving, vain, prideful creatures, a transformation even God cannot reverse by an act of will or power. This is not punishment by God, but something rather different, the natural consequences of our own conduct and character. God does not initiate and control this transformation, but laments it. The whole story of Jesus is in fact the expression of a divine love calling upon us to reverse it.

But is there the other kind of punishment too, not self-inflicted but inflicted by God? Does God in fact punish some people beyond the punishment they inflict upon themselves? If not, why does Jesus talk as he does about those who will not be able to enter the narrow door, try as they might? If so, what are we to think or say or do about this fact?

8

The Passion According to John

There follows one of the great passages of the New Testament, John's account of the Crucifixion of Jesus and the events that led up to it. This is the central Christian story.

How can we connect to it? Is it true, for example, and if so in what sense? What can this story of an unjust execution two thousand years ago mean to us now?

Where are we in this story?

The Gospel of John 18:1—19:42

After Jesus had spoken these words, he went out with his disciples across the Kidron valley to a place where there was a garden, which he and his disciples entered. Now Judas, who betrayed him, also knew the place, because Jesus often met there with his disciples. So Judas brought a detachment of soldiers together with police from the chief priests and the Pharisees, and they came there with lanterns and torches and weapons.

Then Jesus, knowing all that was to happen to him, came forward and asked them, "Whom are you looking for?" They answered, "Jesus of Nazareth." Jesus replied, "I am he." Judas, who betrayed him, was standing with them. When Jesus said to them, "I am he," they stepped back and fell to the ground. Again he asked them, "Whom are you looking for?" And they said, "Jesus of Nazareth." Jesus answered, "I told you that I am he. So if you are looking for me, let these men go." This was to fulfill the word that he had spoken, "I did not lose a single one of those whom you gave me." Then Simon Peter, who had a sword, drew it, struck the high priest's slave, and cut off his right ear. The slave's name was Malchus. Jesus said to Peter, "Put your sword back into its sheath. Am I not to drink the cup that the Father has given me?"

So the soldiers, their officer, and the Jewish police arrested Jesus and bound him. First they took him to Annas, who was the father-in-law of Caiaphas, the high priest that year. Caiaphas was the one who had advised the Jews that it was better to have one person die for the people.

Simon Peter and another disciple followed Jesus. Since that disciple was known to the high priest, he went with Jesus into the courtyard of the high priest, but Peter was standing outside at the gate. So the other disciple, who was known to the high priest, went out, spoke to the woman who guarded the gate, and brought Peter in. The woman said to Peter, "You are not also one of this man's disciples, are you?" He said, "I am not." Now the slaves and the police had made a charcoal fire because it was cold, and they were standing around it and warming themselves. Peter also was standing with them and warming himself.

Then the high priest questioned Jesus about his disciples and about his teaching. Jesus answered, "I have spoken openly to the world; I have always taught in synagogues and in the temple, where all the Jews come together. I have said nothing in secret. Why do you ask me? Ask those who heard what I said to them; they know what I said." When he had said this, one of the police standing nearby struck Jesus on the face, saying, "Is that how you answer the high priest?" Jesus answered, "If I have spoken wrongly, testify to the wrong. But if I have spoken rightly, why do you strike me?" Then Annas sent him bound to Caiaphas the high priest.

Now Simon Peter was standing and warming himself. They asked him, "You are not also one of his disciples, are you?" He denied it and said, "I am not." One of the slaves of the high priest, a relative of the man whose ear Peter had cut off, asked, "Did I not see you in the garden with him?" Again Peter denied it, and at that moment the cock crowed.

Then they took Jesus from Caiaphas to Pilate's headquarters. It was early in the morning. They themselves did not enter the headquarters, so as to avoid ritual defilement and to be able to eat the Passover. So Pilate went out to them and said, "What accusation do you bring against this man?" They answered, "If this man were not a criminal, we would not have handed him over to you." Pilate said to them, "Take him yourselves and judge him according to your law." The Jews replied, "We are not permitted to put anyone to death." (This was to fulfill what Jesus had said when he indicated the kind of death he was to die.)

Then Pilate entered the headquarters again, summoned Jesus, and asked him, "Are you the King of the Jews?" Jesus answered, "Do you ask this on your own, or did others tell you about me?" Pilate replied, "I am not a Jew, am I? Your own nation and the chief priests have handed you over to me. What have you done?" Jesus answered, "My kingdom is not from this world. If my kingdom were from this world, my followers would be fighting to keep me from being handed over to the Jews. But as it is, my kingdom is not from here." Pilate asked him, "So you are a king?" Jesus answered, "You say that I am a king. For this I was born, and for this I came into the world, to testify to the truth. Everyone who belongs to the truth listens to my voice."

Pilate asked him, "What is truth?"

After he had said this, he went out to the Jews again and told them, "I find no case against him. But you have a custom that I release someone for you at the Passover. Do you want me to release for you the King of the Jews?" They shouted in reply, "Not this man, but Barabbas!" Now Barabbas was a bandit.

Then Pilate took Jesus and had him flogged. And the soldiers wove a crown of thorns and put it on his head, and they dressed him in a purple robe. They kept coming up to him, saying, "Hail, King of the Jews!" and striking him on the face. Pilate went out again and said to them, "Look, I am bringing him out to you to let you know that I find no case against him." So Jesus came out, wearing the crown of thorns and the purple robe. Pilate said to them, "Here is the man!" When the chief priests and the police saw him, they shouted, "Crucify him! Crucify him!" Pilate said to them, "Take him yourselves and crucify him; I find no case against him." The Jews answered him, "We have a law, and according to that law he ought to die because he has claimed to be the Son of God."

Now when Pilate heard this, he was more afraid than ever. He entered his headquarters again and asked Jesus, "Where are you from?" But Jesus gave him no answer. Pilate therefore said to him, "Do you refuse to speak to me? Do you not know that I have power to release you, and power to crucify you?" Jesus answered him, "You would have no power over me unless it had been given you from above; therefore the one who handed me over to you is guilty of a greater sin." From then on Pilate tried to release him, but the Jews cried out, "If you release this man, you are no friend of the emperor. Everyone who claims to be a king sets himself against the emperor."

When Pilate heard these words, he brought Jesus outside and sat on the judge's bench at a place called The Stone Pavement, or in Hebrew Gabbatha. Now it was the day of Preparation for the Passover; and it was about noon. He said to the Jews, "Here is your King!" They cried out, "Away with him! Away with him! Crucify him!" Pilate asked them, "Shall I crucify your King?" The chief priests answered, "We have no king but the emperor." Then he handed him over to them to be crucified.

So they took Jesus; and carrying the cross by himself, he went out to what is called The Place of the Skull, which in Hebrew is called Golgotha. There they crucified him, and with him two others, one on either side, with Jesus between them. Pilate also had an inscription written and put on the cross. It read, "Jesus of Nazareth, the King of the Jews." Many of the Jews read this inscription, because the place where Jesus was crucified was near the city; and it was written in Hebrew, in Latin, and in Greek. Then the chief priests of the Jews said to Pilate, "Do not write, 'The King of the Jews,' but, 'This man said, I am King of the Jews.'" Pilate answered, "What I have written I have written." When the soldiers had crucified Jesus, they took his clothes and divided them into four parts, one for each soldier. They also took his tunic; now the tunic was seamless, woven in one piece from the top. So they said to one another, "Let us not tear it, but cast lots for it to see who will get it." This was to fulfill what the scripture says, "They divided my clothes among themselves, and for my clothing they cast lots." And that is what the soldiers did.

Meanwhile, standing near the cross of Jesus were his mother, and his mother's sister, Mary the wife of Clopas, and Mary

Magdalene. When Jesus saw his mother and the disciple whom he loved standing beside her, he said to his mother, "Woman, here is your son." Then he said to the disciple, "Here is your mother." And from that hour the disciple took her into his own home.

After this, when Jesus knew that all was now finished, he said (in order to fulfill the scripture), "I am thirsty." A jar full of sour wine was standing there. So they put a sponge full of the wine on a branch of hyssop and held it to his mouth. When Jesus had received the wine, he said, "It is finished." Then he bowed his head and gave up his spirit.

Since it was the day of Preparation, the Jews did not want the bodies left on the cross during the sabbath, especially because that sabbath was a day of great solemnity. So they asked Pilate to have the legs of the crucified men broken and the bodies removed. Then the soldiers came and broke the legs of the first and of the other who had been crucified with him. But when they came to Jesus and saw that he was already dead, they did not break his legs. Instead, one of the soldiers pierced his side with a spear, and at once blood and water came out. (He who saw this has testified so that you also may believe. His testimony is true, and he knows that he tells the truth.) These things occurred so that the scripture might be fulfilled, "None of his bones shall be broken." And again another passage of scripture says, "They will look on the one whom they have pierced."

After these things, Joseph of Arimathea, who was a disciple of Jesus, though a secret one because of his fear of the Jews, asked Pilate to let him take away the body of Jesus. Pilate gave him permission; so he came and removed his body. Nicodemus, who had at first come to Jesus by night, also came, bringing a mixture of myrrh and aloes, weighing about a hundred pounds. They took the body of Jesus and wrapped it with the spices in linen cloths, according to the burial custom of the Jews. Now there was a garden in the place where he was crucified, and in the garden there was a new tomb in which no one had ever been laid. And so, because it was the Jewish day of Preparation, and the tomb was nearby, they laid Jesus there.

The Passion According to John

ST. ANDREW'S CHURCH, MARCH 25, 2005

May the words of my mouth and the meditations of my heart be always acceptable in thy sight, O Lord, my strength and my redeemer.

TODAY IS OF COURSE Good Friday, the day we experience the death and loss of Christ. In the story we just heard, and enacted, Jesus suffers and dies, leaving us behind as he left his friends and family. It is the most solemn day of our year, marked by our sense of desolation and bereftness.

It happens that Good Friday was the day my mother died, several decades ago. In the following years, which were a time when I did not go to church much, I would always go on Good Friday, when I could allow myself to experience again my own sense of personal bereftness.

I was bereft not only of my mother, whose death was a wound and scar, but of something else, though I had no name for it. What made me aware that I was feeling something I had not expected was my horrified response, each time, to the fact that on Good Friday the altar had been stripped of everything that marked it as an altar, indeed that the church, like this church today, had been stripped of everything that made it a church. It was as though jackbooted totalitarians had taken control of the whole world, and abolished forever the very idea of a church, turning the buildings into empty hulks, indistinguishable from warehouses. This was to me, even in my relatively alienated state, utterly intolerable and a source of immense sadness.

I was aware that I was imagining life without the Church, and I was surprised at my sense of desolation. But more deeply, I think, without knowing it, I was imagining life without Jesus, without God. At a level of which I was totally unaware, this was the loss I grieved. Though I could only dimly hear and feel it, this sense of desolation was in fact a kind of call to me, as the Passion as a whole is a call to us all.

Loss—the loss of Christ, the loss of God—is what we are asked to contemplate today, and it is a loss that none of us can bear. It is to imagine an existence without meaning, without love, without the very source of life. This is indeed our day of bereftness.

The most appropriate response we can make to this Gospel is no doubt simply to feel and experience the loss. That is mainly what we are all doing today, just feeling it, without analyzing it, perhaps without even naming it.

But it is also natural and perhaps proper to think about and to question what we are experiencing. Why is it that we must suffer this loss every year, even for a day or two? And why is it that Jesus had to die in such a way in the first place, by humiliation and by torture? For non-Christians, as Saint Paul said, Jesus' death by crucifixion is either a scandal, as it is to the Jews, or foolishness, as it is to the Greeks. Our religion seems to be based on violence and blood. What kind of God is this, who dies this way?

It would have been perfectly possible, after all, for Jesus to appear among us as a smiling benign presence of infinite wisdom and virtue, like the Buddha, teaching us moral lessons—showing us how to live—and then to die a peaceful death that could have been a model for us all. Or he might have simply ascended to heaven without dying at all. Or, at the very least, if for some reason he had to die on the cross, he could have undergone his Crucifixion without pain, demonstrating his superiority to suffering and thus revealing his divine nature and power to the world.

"If you are the Son of God, why do you not save yourself?" In the Synoptic Gospels this question is uttered as a sadistic taunt (e.g., Matthew 27:40), but it is a real question nonetheless, asked over and over by critics of Christianity from the beginning. Why should Jesus die, and in this way? And why at our hands? There is a sense in which this is indeed an irrational or scandalous way to imagine the Deity, as dying among thieves and murderers.

It is sometimes said that Jesus is dying for our sins, which are so monumental that only the death of God can be an adequate sacrifice or compensation for them. But this has always seemed to me too abstract and theoretical, too quantitative and rigid, to serve as an explanation. It is true that we are sinful and fallen; but it is not clear why anyone at all has to pay for our sins in such a tit-for-tat way. This sounds like a primitive view of the Deity, vengeful and cruel, driven by a rigid conception of justice. Why could Jesus not just present himself to us as the God of Love and let us follow him?

Of course no one can hope fully to explain the Crucifixion, but I do think that one thing the story of the Passion is telling us is that Jesus is not the kind of smiling, serene, moralistic teacher of wisdom people sometimes take him to be: the prophet who offers a new ethical vision and a promise of life above suffering. Quite the opposite: Jesus knows that suffering is part of our life, and he has chosen to share it, to be present among us, to enter human history, and to live life on our terms—loving, living, suffering, dying.

Jesus is not interested in sanitizing or prettifying or sentimentalizing or otherwise denying the conditions of human life, but in facing them, with us and for us, and facing them more fully than any of us can do. We tend to deny the reality of suffering whenever we can, certainly the suffering of others and sometimes even our own. We act most of the time as though nothing really bad will ever happen to us, and when it does we tend to slip away and hide, as though our suffering betrays a shameful weakness. Jesus does not hide or deny his suffering or ours. He endures all that we endure, and more; for he chooses it, submits to it voluntarily, and does so with a kind of knowledge and directness and clarity that we can never achieve.

Jesus knows, that is, what it is to suffer as human beings suffer, for he suffers that way himself, and before our eyes. Jesus is also telling us—if we can hear it—that when we suffer he is there, in our suffering, with us. I think it is in fact in large part to tell us, to show us, that we are not alone in our grief or misery but known and cared for, that Christ dies on the Cross. He is calling us to face the real nature of our existence, including the reality both of suffering and of love.

For suffering is an essential part of human life and the Gospel is telling us that Jesus knows this. He knows the suffering you endure if you lose your job; or if your marriage dissolves in acrimonious divorce; or if you learn that your child has a fatal illness; or if you are told over the phone that your spouse has been killed in a car crash; or if you suffer the ravages of cancer or of Alzheimer's disease or ALS; or if you are a child abandoned by your parents, or abused by a teacher or priest; or if you are raped, or beaten and left to die; or if you are hungry and homeless, without a friend in the world; or if you experience lifelong humiliation and abuse, or psychological torment.

Each of these things has in fact been suffered by people in this congregation, or by people we know elsewhere. Such terrible wounds and traumas and sufferings are a part of our life. What this Gospel is telling us is that our God both knows our suffering and is present with us in it.

We will suffer but not alone; and we need no longer be afraid. Perhaps we can begin to learn, what Christ knows, that only the person who knows what suffering is can experience the reality of joy. This is what the Gospel is telling us.

This is not a God who lives on a mountain, or in the sky, or beneath the sea, or in a storm or even in a still small voice in the wilderness: he lives with us, and shares the painful and mortal conditions of our lives. Christ is with those tortured in Guantánamo, or Saudi Arabia, or Afghanistan, and with the torturers too, weeping for what they do to themselves as well as for what they do to their victims.

It is important that the Gospel says all this not in some abstract and theoretical way, as a matter of dogma or doctrine, but in a heart-wrenching story told in dramatic and significant detail. This great story lives in our minds when we hear it, and when we remember it. When it does so, when our feelings and imaginations are engaged with sympathy for Christ and sorrow for ourselves, something else is happening too, a kind of miracle: Jesus himself is present in our response to his suffering, and in our response to the suffering of others too. That is what our sense of desolation and loss really means. Jesus not only enters human history, as I said a moment ago; in our experience of loss and sorrow and sympathy he enters our hearts, which can become his lodging place forever.

Our sense of desolation and bereftness is in this sense a profound work of grace, a call to life for which we should be ever grateful.

Amen

Judas betrays Jesus, the ultimate crime. Dante will put him in the bottom circle of hell. But Judas had been chosen by Jesus as a disciple. Jesus loved him. What was Judas doing when he betrayed Jesus? Does it help us understand Judas to ask what we ourselves were doing on the occasions when we have betrayed Jesus, in our moments of supreme selfishness, wanton destructiveness, blind carelessness, deliberate evil?

Peter denies Jesus three times, an act so human as to touch every heart that reads it. Somehow the feeling of pathos is made even more intense when we are told that he is warming himself by a charcoal fire on this cold, dark night. We have all warmed ourselves in the cold, and we have all denied Jesus. Is Peter's denial a response to what he feels to be his abandonment by Jesus, his sense of isolation in a world without meaning? Can our denials be explained in the same way?

9

The Parable of the Sower

The parable of the sower is a familiar one: some of the seed cast by the sower falls on the path, some on rocky ground, some among the thorns, and some upon good soil. The seed that falls on the path or the rocky ground or among the thorns does not prosper, but that which falls on the good soil flourishes and bears good fruit.

What does this story mean? In one sense it is obvious: it is not about seeds and plants, but about the Word being sown in us, and it tell us that it would be best if we could be good soil so that the seed could flourish in us.

But how are we to become good soil? Is this a matter of human choice? What happens to those who are not good soil, and what does it mean?

Where are we in this parable?

The Gospel of Matthew 13:1–9, 18–23

That same day Jesus went out of the house and sat beside the sea. Such great crowds gathered around him that he got into a boat and sat there, while the whole crowd stood on the beach. And he told them many things in parables, saying, "Listen! A sower went out to sow. And as he sowed, some seeds fell on the path, and the birds came and ate them up. Other seeds fell on rocky ground, where they did not have much soil, and they sprang up quickly, since they had no depth of soil. But when the sun rose, they were scorched; and since they had no root, they withered away. Other seeds fell among thorns, and the thorns grew up and choked them. Other seeds fell on good soil and brought forth grain, some a hundredfold, some sixty, some thirty. Let anyone with ears listen!"

[Now Jesus is speaking to the disciples privately.] "Hear then the parable of the sower. When anyone hears the word of the kingdom and does not understand it, the evil one comes and snatches away what is sown in the heart; this is what was sown on the path. As for what was sown on rocky ground, this is the one who hears the word and immediately receives it with joy; yet such a person has no root, but endures only for a while, and when trouble or persecution arises on account of the word, that person immediately falls away. As for what was sown among thorns, this is the one who hears the word, but the cares of the world and the lure of wealth choke the word, and it yields nothing. But as for what was sown on good soil, this is the one who hears the word and understands it, who indeed bears fruit and yields, in one case a hundredfold, in another sixty, and in another thirty."

ST. ANDREW'S CHURCH, JULY 10, 2005

May the words of my mouth and the meditations of my heart be always acceptable in thy sight, O Lord, my strength and my redeemer.

IN THE FAMOUS PASSAGE we just heard, Jesus first tells the crowd the parable of the sower, then explains it in detail to his disciples. Some of the seed, he says, falls on the path and is eaten by birds; this image refers to those who do not understand the Word, which the Evil One snatches from them. Some of the seed falls on rocky ground, where it sprouts quickly but then dies in the heat of the sun; this is an image of the person who receives the Word but has no root within him and thus quickly falls away when he faces the costs that the new life entails, especially the cost of persecution. Some of the seed falls among thorns, which choke its growth; this is an image of the person who receives the Word, but whose ambitions and worldly cares prevent its growth. Some of the seed falls on good soil; this is an image of the one who hears the Word and understands it and lives it out with single-minded courage.

I have to say that Jesus' explanation of his parable seems to me a little odd. It makes the story sound rather mechanical, doctrinal, and authoritarian, very different from Jesus' usual parables, which live in the mind as deeply ambiguous and often troubling occasions for reflection. But as Jesus explains it, this one seems to be using a language of images to say something that could be said perfectly well in direct terms, and which is to boot rather obvious: that people do respond differently to the Word sent forth in Jesus and by Jesus—some better and some worse.

What is more, Jesus does not really tell us exactly what this fact means for us. He seems to be saying that those represented by the good soil are saved, everyone else condemned. This is maybe all right if you are the good soil, but not so good if you are not—and which of us knows what kind of soil we are?

As he explains it then, the parable raises, but does not really address, profoundly uncomfortable questions about the nature of salvation.

Do you have the feeling that the condemnation the story implies is unfair? It is not based upon what someone chooses to do or to be, but upon their basic nature. "How can I help being rocky soil, or crowded by thorns, or exposed to the birds?" someone might reasonably ask. "This is how you made me!" The story seems to be saying that what God approves or disapproves is not a matter of virtue in the usual sense—not a matter of choice or discipline or struggle or decision—but of circumstance or identity. Some people are just better soil than others. That is the way it is. Nothing we do can change that.

This to me at least is not an attractive way to think, nor one I associate with the way Jesus usually talks. Suppose I do have trouble understanding the Word: Is that a moral fault? Maybe I am slow of mind, or have difficulty paying attention; or, much more serious, perhaps I have been abused or neglected as a child in ways that make it very difficult indeed for me to have any trust at all, let alone be able to accept Jesus' proclamation of a God of love. Or maybe I am by nature quick-witted and enthusiastic, but just lack the reservoir of strength, the deep self-confidence, that makes it possible to endure in the face of a serious threat. Or perhaps I have real cares that overwhelm me, say cares for my children or parents, or for an ill spouse. Are these things really my fault? Or is the condemnation Jesus speaks of not based upon fault? Can Jesus really be saying about me, or you, in all these cases: "Tough for you; what I want is good soil, and you do not measure up?"

This does not fit with my sense of Jesus as infinitely loving and understanding and forgiving. Yet he does tell pretty much the same story and gives pretty much the same explanation in all three of the synoptic Gospels. Moreover, what he says is based upon an obvious truth, that people do respond differently to the Word, and reflect different kinds and degrees of spiritual capacity. So what we are to do about this passage?

At the very least, I think, we should recognize that we do not know who is the better soil, who the worse, especially with respect to ourselves. To claim to know who is saved and who is not is a dangerous presumption in any human being, at any time. After all, it may not be the openly devout Episcopalian who comes to church on Sunday and says his prayers regularly, and even gives away a tenth of his income, who is in fact the best and deepest soil for the Word. Maybe the person tortured by doubt and guilt, captured by an addiction he cannot break, acting out his sense of worthlessness in destructive ways, is closer to the kingdom of God than the rest of us: for he may be more fully aware of his own defects, his own need for God and for forgiveness. God may listen most deeply and lovingly not to the socially well-adjusted person who has always done what is expected of him or her, but to the one who tries and tries to love, who tries and tries to accept love, and finds that he or she cannot do it.

Perhaps we need to rethink the parable itself. Perhaps the emphasis on salvation and condemnation, though it does seem to be present, is not its main point. Is there another way to imagine it?

We could start with the fact that Jesus has recently sent his disciples out into the world to preach and to heal. They are sent "like sheep into the midst of wolves," as he puts it (Matthew 10:16). This suggests that the point of this parable, at least as Jesus explains it to his disciples, may actually not be to make proclamations about who is saved and who is not, but to help the disciples shape their expectations about the ministry to which they have been called. Maybe his object is not to say anything about who will be saved, who condemned, but to tell the disciples what to expect of others when they themselves try to spread the Word: that what they say will often fall on deaf ears, or be the occasion of brief and insubstantial enthusiasm, or be choked off by other cares. Maybe Jesus is here mainly concerned not with the fate of the different types of people but with the fate of the Word.

For a comparison think what you might say to a young person starting off as a teacher, in school or college. You would warn them that not everyone will hear what they have to say, or understand it; and those who do hear and understand will not all like it. People are different, and respond to the same person, to the same message, differently. "So do not be downhearted at what seem to be your failures," you would say. "This is what the world is like."

What is true of students is true of all of us, and true of children, of friends, of colleagues, even of spouses. None of us is always able to listen and respond to another person, even a person speaking truth or love from their heart. Sometimes we don't hear or understand, or don't care, or just can't focus our attention. Jesus is telling not only his disciples, but all of us, in all of our relationships, that a profound and permanent imperfection is the lot of humanity, not only in our efforts to speak and to listen, but much more deeply, in every aspect of life. It is part of our Fall of into sin.

This is a central problem, for all of us, in all our lives. We find that we are sometimes the path, sometimes the rocky soil, sometimes the thorny soil, and sometimes the good soil, in relation not only to what Jesus says, but to what anyone says: our children, our husbands and wives, our friends, our teachers, our students, the authors we read. Although this is not Jesus' main concern here, we are equally defective as speakers, in trying to say what is in our hearts. Our words turn to ashes in our mouths as we utter cliché after cliché. And we are defective in our conduct too, when we find ourselves failing, again and again, to realize the good intentions we thought we had.

Maybe the real question Jesus is addressing here is how to live with the fact that it is difficult in the extreme to reach the hearts and minds of people who are made as we are: deaf and preoccupied and distractible, damaged and hurt and misguided, insistent on our wrongheaded views of what we need and should want—all of which makes us incapable of hearing Jesus' own direct and simple message of hope and trust and love. In a world where others are like this too, how are we to try to speak the Word, how are we to try to live it out?

A wise old teacher once told me that she had learned to waste as little time as possible in wishing that the students who came to her class were better educated, more competent, or more willing to engage than in fact they were. Her job was to work with them as they came to her. And that is I think what Jesus is telling the disciples and us as well: the fact is that some will hear, others not, some respond, others not, some keep at it, others not. You are not to become disheartened by what seem to be your failures, in part because they are necessary, in part because you cannot confidently tell your failures from your successes.

So don't worry about who is saved and who is not; no one is good soil, or rocky soil, all the time. Jesus knows that we are sometimes one sort of soil, sometimes another, not always the same. It is not some of us who cannot hear the Word, but all of us, most of the time. But we are to keep on, trying to hear the Word—trying to speak the Word, trying to live the Word—in the knowledge that we will often fail; but we are not to do this timidly or in fear, but in hope and confidence, as we are told in the beautiful words that Isaiah gives to the Source of all Blessing:

> For as the rain and snow come down from heaven, and do not return there until they have watered the earth, making it bring forth and sprout, giving seed to the sower and bread to the eater, so shall my word be that goes forth from my mouth; it shall not return to me empty, but it shall accomplish that which I purpose, and succeed in the thing for which I sent it. (Isaiah 55:10-11)

Amen

Why does Jesus give the explanation of the parable only to the twelve disciples, not to the people at large? When asked by the disciples why he is speaking to the people in parables without explaining what he means, he says, *"To you it has been given to know the secrets of the kingdom of heaven, but to them it has not been given"* (Matthew 13:11).

What can this possibly mean? Jesus says that it fulfills a prophecy of Isaiah, beginning, "You will indeed listen, but never understand, and you will indeed look, but never perceive" (Matthew 13:14–15).

But why would Jesus want to fulfill that prophecy? And what has this secrecy to do with his role and mission, which is apparently to make the Word known as clearly and powerfully as possible?

10

"Get Thee Behind Me, Satan!"

This passage from Matthew contains the famous moment in which Jesus says to Peter the words quoted above, "Get thee behind me Satan!"[1]

What would bring Jesus to speak in such a way to a disciple, especially to the one he calls the rock upon which his church will be founded? What does he mean by it, for Peter and for us?

Where are we in this passage?

The Gospel of Matthew 16:21–27

From that time on, Jesus began to show his disciples that he must go to Jerusalem and undergo great suffering at the hands of the elders and chief priests and scribes, and be killed, and on the third day be raised. And Peter took him aside and began to rebuke him, saying, "God forbid it, Lord! This must never happen to you." But he turned and said to Peter, "Get behind me, Satan! You are a stumbling block to me; for you are setting your mind not on divine things but on human things."

Then Jesus told his disciples, "If any want to become my followers, let them deny themselves and take up their cross and follow me. For those who want to save their life will lose it, and those who lose their life for my sake will find it. For what will it profit

---

1. In modern translations the word *thee*, which appears in the King James Version, is left out. I restored it here because of its familiarity and force.

them if they gain the whole world but forfeit their life? Or what will they give in return for their life?

"For the Son of Man is to come with his angels in the glory of his Father, and then he will repay everyone for what has been done."

The Church of the Mediator, August 28, 2005

May the words of my mouth and the meditations of my heart be always acceptable to thee, O Lord, my strength and my redeemer.

In the first part of the passage we have just heard from the Gospel of Matthew, Jesus starts to tell his disciples what is coming: that he will suffer at the hands of the authorities, and be crucified, and then rise again on the third day.

He is of course preparing his friends for what he knows is going to happen, and his task is not an easy one. This is not the kind of thing you can say once, and be done with it. No one can absorb quickly the fact or prospect of the death of a beloved person; and as for the idea of his being raised up on the third day, contrary to all human experience, that must have taken a good deal of repetition indeed. That is why Matthew says Jesus "began" to explain to his disciples what was coming.

Peter reveals that he for one does not really understand what Jesus is saying, for he rebukes him, saying in essence, "Let this never happen to you!"

Jesus does not allow Peter to go on, but if he did you can imagine Peter saying something like this:

> Don't do this, Lord. It does not have to happen. We can escape from Jerusalem any time, and go back to the north where we come from. They will not follow you there. And consider this: if you die now you will be abandoning your friends and the whole purpose of your life. If you stay alive you may have fifty more years of teaching and healing, fifty more years of friendship and love, fifty more years in which to establish your Church. You are only thirty-three years old! Your work is not done. If you die now what good will you do anyone but the Roman government and the establishment in Jerusalem? You are here on a mission! Don't give it up!

Not a bad argument, not at all. We can see why Jesus would be tempted by it—tempted to the point of saying to Peter, *"Get thee behind me, Satan!"* Jesus is in a sense right to call Peter that, for Satan in the New Testament is a tempter—he tempts Jesus himself—and at the moment Peter is also a tempter, tempting Jesus to take a different and easier course of action.

Jesus tells Peter that in giving this advice he has been setting his mind on human things, not divine things. This does not seem quite fair: Peter could say in response that while he has been thinking partly about himself, he has also been thinking about divine things, especially about the great mission Jesus has been given, which he will be giving up if he dies.

So what can Jesus mean when he says that Peter is thinking of "human things"? He does not mean that Peter is thinking of wealth and power or anything like that, but I think something a little different, and more complicated, and more accurate, which might be put this way.

Jesus himself seems to have a conflict, a conflict between highly persuasive arguments for what seems like prudence, such as the ones I have attributed to Peter, and a feeling or awareness, which perhaps he cannot quite explain, that he is called to do something unexpected that is much, much more painful. I think he has the sense that he has a role that is not determined wholly by himself, in a life story the shape of which he does not control, which he may not fully understand, and with a meaning he can only dimly glimpse.

Yet somewhere at the center of his being he knows that the story he cannot quite grasp is to be his story, and that its meaning is to be his meaning: he is the one who is to die for the world, and rise again. This secret sense of call, dimly perceived, is the divine thing of which Peter is not thinking.

Something a little like this sometimes happens to us too. We, too, sometimes have the sense that we have a role, not wholly chosen by ourselves, in a life story the shape of which we do not completely understand, with a meaning we can only dimly glimpse. When we feel this tension, Jesus helps us name it: a conflict between human things and divine things.

It works like this. Usually we think of ourselves as aiming for control of our lives, making decisions to produce what we desire. Often this way of doing things seems to work all right. We are proud of our capacity to achieve our ends in the world.

But sometimes we find that the decisions we make, for what seem at the time very good reasons—to move to Michigan or Colorado; to go to college, or not to do so; to take up this line of work or that; to date this person or that one; to join the band in high school or to try out for the track team—do not work out the way we expect, not at all. We are often disappointed, sometimes bitterly so. The job is dull; the weather is impossible; the commute is killing; the marriage collapses. Where we planned for happiness we face pain and loss and unhappiness. This is part of human life.

Yet sometime, maybe only years later, we may come to see that the "bad" decision actually made a kind of sense of its own, different from what we expected or intended. The very pain, or loss, or disappointment, the big mistake, may have been an important part of a life story, a part we would never have chosen consciously but which may have been right all along.

As it is Jesus' role to die on the cross for the world and to rise again, it may be our role to experience the pain and tragedy of a bad marriage, or the frustration of bad work, or the sense of alienation that comes from living in the wrong place, among the wrong people. It is right for us to suffer these things, not for their own sake, but for what they in the end can teach us: a deeper understanding of our own frailty; a greater awareness of our own susceptibility to deep mistakes; a more acute consciousness of our own need for forgiving love; and a deeper sense of the call to be servants of God, not of ourselves.

What Jesus is telling us (and Peter) is that when we hear within us the stirring of a call, we are to pay attention to it, for it may be a divine thing; we should not, as we usually do, think solely of our interests and needs, and of strategies to protect and advance them—for these are human things.

In the second part of the passage, Jesus turns from Peter to his disciples as a group and gives further content to what he means by the things of God. *"If any want to become my followers,"* he says, *"let them deny themselves and take up their cross and follow me. For those who want to save their life will lose it; and those who lose it for my sake will find it. For what will it profit them if they gain the whole world, but forfeit their life?"* Here he is continuing the conversation he had with Peter, telling the disciples that they must learn to accept, as he must too, the call that leads them into more painful but richer life.

When Jesus says, to them and to us, that we must take up our cross and follow him, he does not mean that we all must be crucified. But he does seem to mean that in order to become fully ourselves, to allow our lives and souls to realize their full identity, we need to do something, which here he expresses when he says, *"If any want to become my followers, let them deny themselves . . . "*

What he means by "deny" is connected I think with what he meant when he told Peter "Get thee behind me, Satan." For Jesus was then saying to Peter something like this: "Stop tempting me into thinking that I am, and should be, in control of the fundamental shape of my life." Now he is telling the disciples, and us, something similar: that the part of the self that seeks to control all aspects of our lives and to manage decisions in a way that is calculated to meet our desires, needs to yield to something else. The things of man need to yield to the things of God.

This is hard to contemplate, for we function out of the controlling side of the self almost all the time—the part that wants to get high grades, or win at sports, or make money, or get a job with prestige, or to be sure our insurance is up to date, or to get the best deal on a car loan, or to have the nicest vacation at the lowest price, and so on, and on, and on. For this part of us, life itself *is* a kind of control: the more we control, the more we think we live.

But when Jesus tells us to deny ourselves and take up our cross he is telling us that to be full human beings we must relinquish our efforts at control; this is what he means when he says his disciple must be ready to lose his "life." Instead, we should learn to trust what he calls "divine things": the force of goodness that flows like a river through all things. We should learn to trust life itself. This will in fact save our lives.

This is obviously what Jesus did. If he had accepted the advice I attributed to Peter, and lived to a ripe old age in Galilee, to die say of pneumonia or in a farm accident at age eighty, he would in one sense have lived longer; but in another, he could never have attained the kind of life he achieved by dying as he did, a life that among other things brings him here in this little church in Michigan, nearly two thousand years later, where he is present in our common life, in our prayers, and in the Eucharist we are about to celebrate.

So with Peter we are told to listen for and to follow the call from God; with the disciples we are told to give up our desire for constant control and to learn instead to trust in the great gift and mystery of life. But these things are much easier said than done. How are we to know whether the inner call we hear is from God; whether our apparent mistakes were actually part of a larger and positive plan; whether our rational and controlling impulses are leading us, this time, in the right or wrong direction? Are we in danger of giving up control too much, of trusting the wrong things, so that we will just drift, the victims of destructive forces?

There are no easy answers to these questions. Our comfort is that they were also real and hard for Jesus—this is why he got so angry at Peter when he interfered with his effort to face them. The best we can do is to try to face them too, in faith and prayer, knowing that when we do so we are not alone.

When we make decisions, as when we suffer afflictions, we can try to listen for a call from the deepest source of meaning in the universe, and try to live it out—even when this leads to loss or pain or suffering, even when we do not understand it—and try to do so in the faith that it will ultimately have significance, in our own lives, and in the lives of others, beyond what we can know or imagine.

Amen

Who is Peter, and why does Jesus call him the rock upon which he will found his church?

In many passages in the Gospels, Peter's extraordinary character shines through what we read, even two thousand years later and in another language. He is utterly sincere, impulsive, and enthusiastic; he bites off more than he can chew; he seeks to face the full truth.

So in this passage he dares to rebuke Jesus. Elsewhere we are told that when Jesus wanted to wash his feet, Peter at first refused—"I should wash *your* feet," he said—but when Jesus told him it was necessary to salvation, he said, in effect, "Wash the rest of me too" (John 13:9). Later Peter told Jesus he would never deny him, and then did so, three times in one night. When he sees the risen Jesus on the beach he leaps into the water. When he sees Jesus walking on the water, he tries to walk across the water to meet him.

He is an extraordinary, paradoxical figure of deep humanity. He has both remarkable strengths and remarkable failings. Is it somehow the *combination* of these strengths and failings that leads Jesus to call him a rock—more of a rock perhaps than if he had strengths alone?

This is a remarkable thought, and it leads to the question: Might our failings and our strengths, working together, make us rocks too?

11

The Laborers in the Vineyard

In this passage, the Gospel presents one of its greatest challenges to our sense of fairness and justice. In the parable Jesus tells, those laborers who are taken on at the last moment of the day, and who worked maybe an hour or even less, are paid exactly the same as the laborers who worked in the field all day in the blazing sun. This is in direct violation of our view of what constitutes a proper reward for labor. Yet Jesus says that this is an image of the kingdom of heaven.

How can that possibly be? What kind of justice is this from a just God?

Where are we in this story?

The Gospel of Matthew 20:1–16

"For the kingdom of heaven is like a landowner who went out early in the morning to hire laborers for his vineyard. After agreeing with the laborers for the usual daily wage, he sent them into his vineyard. When he went out about nine o'clock, he saw others standing idle in the marketplace; and he said to them, 'You also go into the vineyard, and I will pay you whatever is right.' So they went. When he went out again about noon and about three o'clock, he did the same. And about five o'clock he went out and found others standing around; and he said to them, 'Why are you standing here idle all day?' They said to him, 'Because no one has hired us.' He said to them, 'You also go into the vineyard.'

"When evening came, the owner of the vineyard said to his manager, 'Call the laborers and give them their pay, beginning with the last and then going to the first.' When those hired about five o'clock came, each of them received the usual daily wage. Now when the first came, they thought they would receive more; but each of them also received the usual daily wage. And when they received it, they grumbled against the landowner, saying, 'These last worked only one hour, and you have made them equal to us who have borne the burden of the day and the scorching heat.'

"But he replied to one of them, 'Friend, I am doing you no wrong; did you not agree with me for the usual daily wage? Take what belongs to you and go; I choose to give to this last the same as I give to you. Am I not allowed to do what I choose with what belongs to me? Or are you envious because I am generous?'

"So the last will be first, and the first will be last."

The Church of the Mediator, September 18, 2005

May the words of my mouth and the meditations of my heart be always acceptable in thy sight, O Lord, my strength and my redeemer.

THE PARABLE THAT JESUS tells in today's Gospel seems to run in obvious opposition to our most deeply held assumptions about justice and fairness. We readily understand the complaint of the laborers who were hired in the morning and worked hard in the sun all day, only to find the latecomers paid the same wage they were. For we too assume that we should be paid in proportion to our labor: according to the number of hours worked, or perhaps to the quality of the work, but in some way proportionately to what we do.

Our most fundamental idea of justice and fairness, in fact, is that it consists of a kind of proportion, and this is so with respect both to rewards and to punishments: justice means earning a reward proportionate to our merit or paying a punishment proportionate to our wrong. The same idea governs debts: what I borrowed is what I should pay; if you ask for more, that is not fair to me; if I ask to pay less, that is not fair to you. And with respect to injuries too: if I injure you, I should pay in proportion to the injury, not more or less. For us justice is proportion.

Along with the idea of proportion we have the idea of entitlement: we are entitled to our fair wage, entitled to recover fair damages, entitled to see wrongdoers fairly punished, entitled to pay no more than our debt.

These ideas of justice as proportion and entitlement are deep in human nature, as anyone knows who has experience of a family in which there is more than one child: "Why should he get a larger allowance, just because he is older?" Or: "Why are you giving him a bike when he is six? I did not get one till I was seven!"

We have all heard and taken part in these endless arguments, which assume that the fundamental idea of justice or fairness is some kind of proportion. If you were to practice law, you would see other versions of the same argument constantly emerging: in criminal law, in commercial law, whenever in fact human beings dispute justice. We seek rewards and punishments that meet the standard of proportionality. We argue about exactly what that standard is, and how it should work in particular cases, but the basic idea of proportionality rules our sense of justice.

What Jesus is saying in this parable is profound and radical, and very hard, maybe impossible, to get our minds around. It is that God does not work the way we do. He gives the same amount to people who seem to deserve different amounts, and does so without embarrassment or explanation. He does not deal in proportions or entitlements. In theological terms, for this God "salvation" is not something you earn by being good all your life; it is an act of grace, not proportioned to human effort or merit in any way. Indeed what motivates the landowner's decision to hire the extra workers in the story, each time, is the fact that they cannot find other work. He is responding to their need, not their merit. God's economy is not like our economy, not at all.

Notice that what we are told in this parable about rewards is directly parallel to what we were told last Sunday about forgiveness, which is equally difficult for us to imagine, let alone put into practice (Matthew 18:21–35). We are to forgive those who have sinned against us, as we are told over and over. This kind of forgiveness does not depend upon someone's asking for it, or apologizing, or otherwise humbling themselves to us. It is to be a free and total gift, like Jesus' own forgiveness of those who crucified him.

We can see this right in the language, for the Greek word usually used for "forgiveness" does not have the pious and sanctimonious overtones of the English word. The literal meaning of the Greek word is to "let go," or "release," or "erase"; it is a term of commercial accounting, which might be used this way: "I release you from your obligation," or "I erase your debt," or " I clear your account." We are supposed to do this not in proportion to the wrong or the debt in question, and not in some cases but not others, but to all who have sinned or trespassed against us, including in terrible ways and whether or not they repent. Jesus is telling us that we are to release the world from its obligations to us.

With respect both to the forgiveness of wrongs and to our attitude towards rewards, then, we are being asked to give up the idea of justice for ourselves, and with it the claims it enables us to make upon others. We are to give up our entitlements. We are not to live by proportion, nor should we exact or expect proportion. We are to erase and cancel all debts, give up all claims for redress; we are to accept thankfully what we are given, and to give up the right to complain that it is not enough compared to someone else. We are to live by God's economy, not our economy.

How can this be? How can we make sense of such an image of life? To give up the idea of justice for ourselves, in reward and punishment alike—to live by forgiveness and grace—would be to give up the core of the social self as we know it. I know that I for one cannot do that. Yet this is what we are asked to do.

Maybe we can make a little progress if we start by realizing that the Master in the parable represents God and that what he is really giving the workers is not money, but love, for that is what God gives; and with love he gives "salvation"—whether we mean by that eternal life in heaven or a life now on earth that is led in harmony with the principle of love at the center of the universe.

If we imagine it that way, we can see that we do not really deserve the reward in the first place, and therefore that we really don't want to invoke the ideas of proportion and entitlement after all. For who could possibly deserve salvation? Who could claim a right to God's love? None of us is entitled to that; none of us has virtue that is proportionate to that blessing.

Suppose that you are good all your life, that you go to church and keep the commandments, and give 10 percent of your income to the poor.

Now suppose there is another person, a wastrel, an evil person who has done wrong to others, maybe violent wrong. Just before he dies he comes to see and understand that what he has done is wrong, in all its horror, and begs for forgiveness. As an old poem puts it, in the mouth of a soldier who converted as he fell in battle, "Between the saddle and the ground I mercy sought and mercy found."

Can you really claim superiority to him? Would you argue to God that he should get less than you?

Here is perhaps part of the secret about what is wrong in the way we think when we demand proportion and entitlement. In God's economy, unlike our own, there is no scarcity. It does not hurt me for you to be saved. Quite the opposite: it is a blessing for everyone who is saved that another should also be.

This is the meaning of the famous story about Jonah. After trying without success to evade God's command to go to Nineveh, he accepts his duty and goes there and does what a prophet is supposed to do. As a spokesman for God he announces the doom that awaits this sinful people. The idea is that when the doom comes it will prove God's power (and incidentally confirm Jonah's special access to God's purposes).

But to everyone's enormous surprise the people of Nineveh repent from their hearts, and God decides not to destroy them after all. Jonah feels humiliated as a prophet, because his declaration was not proven true. In a real sense God has let him down. Who will ever take him seriously as a prophet again? In his human economy, this is a grievous wrong. So God teaches Jonah what *his* economy is like: first he gives him a tree for shade, which Jonah enjoys greatly; then he destroys it. When Jonah laments its loss, God says, in essence, "If the tree is precious to you, think how precious the people of Nineveh are to me."

God refuses to apply Jonah's idea of justice, or to think that way; he accepts no argument based on any such vision of justice, or equality, or entitlement, or even professional role; instead, he tries to teach Jonah, and us, the basis of his economy, of his sense of right. It is not proportion or entitlement, but love: as Jonah loves the tree, God loves the people of Nineveh; so too the Master loves the workers, and so we are told that God loves us.

This is God's economy and it can be our economy too. Not that we are capable of limitless love, as God is, but we should be able to see that it does not hurt us if our brother or sister is loved by our parents, or if this poor person is fed and clothed by a rich man. Jesus says the last shall be first, and the first shall be last. He is telling us that in the kingdom of heaven there is no competition, no striving to dominate, no exaction for wrongs, no struggle for scarce benefits.

This is the attitude we are to have towards the things that are normally governed by our economy: rewards and punishments and property and entitlements. All these things are to be made subject to the larger economy of love.

Money is scarce, but love is in principle infinite: every true act of love, or true moment of love, stimulates a loving response, which in turn stimulates other loving responses. We can all see this is true as a matter of ordinary experience in our lives, including our lives in our families and in this church. But the love to which we are called is not just a set of feelings, of affection or concern or delight—though it is all those things—but also a way of acting out of love in the world, and doing so with things that are indeed scarce: money and food and clothing and shelter, and maybe, as Jesus himself shows us, life itself. This is the economy Jesus came to establish, and it is to govern not only our feelings but every aspect of life.

How are we possibly to live that way, broken and incomplete and selfish as we are? We cannot do so perfectly, of course, but we can try; and when we do try, we have Jesus' example before us and his presence with us, and for that we should be constantly and deeply thankful. We know that what matters most in all the world is not scarce, not the proper subject of competition, or complaint, or pride, but freely given to all who turn to him.

Thanks be to God.

Amen

Another way into this passage would be by way of the owner's question, "Are you envious because I am generous?"

Even to put the question shows how unattractive and unjustified such feelings of envy would be, yet lots of us have experienced exactly that kind of envy in ourselves. "She is beautiful, and I am not; he is a good football player, and I am not; she is smart, and I am not; he is genial and likeable, and I am not." How do we respond to such disparities? Often with envy: envy that eats at our heart, drives us into unhappiness, and destroys our capacity to take pleasure in who we can actually be, what we can actually do. Envy prevents us from living fully on the conditions on which the blessings of life are given us.

But some people who are on the losing end of such comparisons do not seem to feel envy at all. What is their secret? How do they avoid this soul-eroding sin?

12

The Transfiguration of Jesus

The story of the Transfiguration of Jesus is one of the strangest passages in the New Testament, a kind of showing-forth of the divine that stretches our imaginations to the utmost. It is certainly difficult for many of us to relate to what we read here, indeed it is hard to make sense of it at all.

How then are we to connect to this passage?

To ask our familiar question, where are we in this story?

The Gospel of Mark 9:2–8

Six days later, Jesus took with him Peter and James and John, and led them up a high mountain apart, by themselves. And he was transfigured before them, and his clothes became dazzling white, such as no one on earth could bleach them. And there appeared to them Elijah with Moses, who were talking with Jesus.

Then Peter said to Jesus, "Rabbi, it is good for us to be here; let us make three dwellings, one for you, one for Moses, and one for Elijah." He did not know what to say, for they were terrified.

Then a cloud overshadowed them, and from the cloud there came a voice, "This is my Son, the Beloved; listen to him!" Suddenly when they looked around, they saw no one with them any more, but only Jesus.

St. Andrew's Church, February 26, 2006

May the words of my mouth and the meditations of my heart be always acceptable in thy sight, O Lord, my strength and my redeemer.

IN CHURCH WE TALK about God all the time, and of course our prayers are addressed to God. But how do we conceive of or imagine God? Who is this God about whom we talk, to whom we pray? This is what the passage we have just heard is about, and it raises perhaps the most fundamental question of a life of faith: How do we perceive and imagine and understand God?

In a sense it is impossible for us to perceive or imagine or understand God. The creator of all that is in the universe must be grander, larger, more powerful, more mysterious than we can possibly capture in a phrase or image. No language, no concepts, can be adequate to his or her description. Jewish practice expresses an awareness of this cosmic inexpressibility in its refusal even to pronounce the name of God. God is beyond us in every way, beyond our imagining. This is what Job learns at the end of the book named for him. His argument that God has treated him unjustly simply wilts when God asserts his magnitude and greatness. "Where were you when I laid the foundations of the earth? Declare, if you have understanding" (Job 38:4).

Our categories collapse in the presence of God. Yet it is an amazing fact of our tradition, Hebrew and Christian alike, that, with God's help, it seeks to find ways to represent God, to imagine God—to imagine God into our lives. Today we have heard two passages that do this, the story of the still small voice that Elijah heard on Sinai (1 Kings 19:9–18) and the Transfiguration of Jesus.

Actually there is a third passage, because both the Elijah story and the Transfiguration make unavoidable allusion to another famous moment in which God reveals himself. I mean of course the moment, also on Sinai, when God reveals the law to Moses and establishes his covenant with his people, Israel.

Let us start with the God of Sinai who spoke to Moses. What was this God like? We are told: "When all the people witnessed the thunder and lightning, the sound of the trumpet, and the mountain smoking, they were afraid, and trembled, and stood at a distance" (Exodus 20:18). When God rewards Moses by giving him the opportunity to behold him, the experience is so transcendent that Moses' face is still glowing when he comes down the mountain.

That is one way the Bible imagines God, and it is rich and enduring, the foundation first of Judaism and then of Christianity: God as the source of all power and authority, God of the mountain and the trumpet and the lightning and the storm.

It is against this image of God that we are invited to read the passage about Elijah. These events take place at a point in the story when Elijah has humiliated the Baal worshippers in the famous fire-lighting contest. (You remember how it goes: Baal cannot light the pile of wood, whatever his worshippers do, but the God of Israel makes it burst into flame even after Elijah has soaked it with water.) King Ahab has now recognized the God of Israel and Elijah thinks the struggle is over.

But Queen Jezebel is unconvinced and seeks to kill Elijah, who goes off into the wilderness in despair, ready to die. He feels utterly alone. He goes to the mountain and spends the night in a cave. He is then told to go out onto the mountain, for the Lord will soon pass by, and he does so. First a wind passes by, then an earthquake, then a fire roaring with destructive power and force. But God is not in those things. God is not experienced that way; rather, in our translation, God is experienced as "the sound of sheer silence," or, in an older translation, as "a still small voice" (1 Kings 19:12). This God is not the triumphal God of Exodus, violent and frightening, but entirely different: quiet, small, hard to see or hear. What this God does is to tell Elijah to go back to the world, to anoint the kings who will restore God's worship in Israel.

It is a story of redemption and rehabilitation, of restoration: the despairing Elijah is revived, and given new life and direction; he in turn will restore and revive Israel.

The third great manifestation of God in today's readings, the third way of imagining God, is of course the famous Transfiguration that Mark describes.

Once again we are on a mountain; Jesus is with his closest friends; without warning, his clothes become dazzling white, whiter than the best bleach could make them, and he is himself "transfigured." This is a term we cannot quite understand—the Greek is related to the term *metamorphosis*, meaning "change of form"—just as we could not quite have understood what was happening if we had been present and seen it all with our own eyes.

Suddenly with Jesus are the human actors in the other two passages, Moses and Elijah. Their appearance suggests that we are to regard Jesus as both the new Moses and the new Elijah, respectively the founder and the restorer of Israel. Then a voice comes from the heavens: *"This is my Son, the Beloved; listen to him!"*

Then the disciples see no one but Jesus, who tells them to keep silence until after he has died and risen.

How is God imagined here? Partly in familiar ways: as the God of the heavens, of power and might, as the one who can transfigure Jesus as he transfigured Moses. But he is also marked here as the father of Jesus; this means that in some way—who can say how?—Jesus is recognized as God too, or part of God, certainly as specially connected to God. Mark does not have our full theological apparatus—no concept of the Trinity for example—but Jesus' sonship is here made explicit. This means that God is present here both ways, as magnificent creator and as human son.

This is an amazing revolution. And Jesus is of course not just any human being; he is one who will, as he says to his disciples, suffer at the hands of the authorities and be killed by them. This is a very different God from the powerful and commanding presence with Moses at Sinai, and very different from the God of Elijah, who orders him to anoint the kings. This is a God who takes on the identity, the conditions of life, of his creatures, including suffering and weakness and death. This is a God who knows what we suffer, for he suffers it too.

But of course it does not stop there. Our God is also a God who will break the bonds of death, and rise again, affirming his power and glory once more. Jesus thus partakes of the magnificence of the God of Moses, the quietness of the God of Elijah, and the humanness of you and me. This is how we are taught by this text to imagine the unimaginable God of the universe. It is beautiful and true.

Amen

Mark sees the story he tells as establishing a connection, almost an identity, between Jesus on the one hand and Moses and Elijah on the other. He is making a claim for the special nature of Jesus in terms that seem to be intended to resonate strongly with his mainly Jewish audience: Jesus is connected with Moses and Elijah, the two great figures from the past; he even surpasses them, for he is addressed from heaven as God's son. That this is a bold claim is obvious. But is true? In what sense, and how do we know?

Here, as often in the Gospels, we face the problem of the omniscient narrator. How does Mark know what happened on the mountain? He certainly was not present at these events. What are we to do in the face of our own ignorance about what Mark knew and how he knew it?

13

Saturday Time

This is my second sermon on the Passion narrative in the Gospel of John. I include it partly to show how differently one person may think about and respond to the same passage at different times.

In saying this I am stressing how particular all of these sermons are: each is a response on a certain day, and in a certain community, to a text that has been read hundreds of thousands of times, every time in its own way differently.

Every Gospel text I have worked on has seemed to yield something completely new to me, something surprising and important. Of course other works can be surprisingly and deeply fruitful, but I mean something different here: the experience I have always had when turning to a Gospel passage upon which I have been asked to preach, however familiar or brief it may be, that it opens up into something deep and new and unexpected. It is almost as though it has been rewritten since the last time I read it. Apparently these texts cannot be exhausted. (To reread the Gospel passage, please turn to chapter 8.)

ST. ANDREW'S CHURCH, GOOD FRIDAY, 2006

May the words of my mouth and the meditations of my heart be always acceptable in thy sight, O Lord, my strength and my redeemer.

TODAY IS OF COURSE Good Friday, the most solemn day of the Christian year, the day on which we remember and reenact the death of Jesus on the cross. This is a story of human cruelty and blindness; of official corruption and cowardice; of pain, despair, and death: How are we to understand it?

One way we might begin to open up its meaning is to imagine ourselves into the story, and we can do that in at least two ways. First, although it is unpleasant, to say the least, we can—and should—see ourselves as the people who killed Jesus. They were human beings like us, after all. Like them we reject Jesus in our own lives, often enough. We have no right to claim superiority to them. These people killed him mainly out of fear, and it is often fear that drives us to do terrible things too.

If we imagine ourselves as the crowd we can see that we are acting as crowds often do, as a kind of lynch mob, driven by our fear. If we imagine ourselves as Pilate, we can see that we are also acting out of fear: fear for our own skin and career, hoping that the problem that interrupts our morning can somehow be made to go away. Notice also that if we imagine ourselves as Pilate we shall find ourselves acting in the way people with power normally do, not directly but through commands given to others. Pilate does not flog Jesus himself, after all, but in a chilling phrase, "had him flogged."

So we are present here as the killers of Jesus, as we just affirmed in our liturgy when we cried out, "Crucify him!" It is not some other people called the Jews who killed Jesus, but we ourselves. We have kept on doing it ever since. Every time we deny the reality of human suffering, or the significance of a moment of love; every time we invite someone to trust us, then break the trust; every time we allow human death or injury or torture to be inflicted in our name, we are killing Jesus.

That is one way to imagine ourselves into this story. But we can also imagine ourselves here in another way, as the disciples and friends of Jesus, as the men and women who love him, as the people for whom he is by far the most important thing that has happened in the world and who have just lost him, they think, forever. As his disciples, we were told earlier by Jesus that all this would occur but we did not really believe it. Now it has happened and we are bereft, in confusion and despair.

The promise implied in Jesus' life seems to be shattered. Even if we did not think that he would be the Messiah who would lead us out of our slavery to the Romans, as some dreamed, we did think that he was an amazing presence on earth, promising us—what he showed us every single day—a new life, a new possibility for human existence, grounded on love not power. It is this man, this presence, who has been destroyed before our eyes, destroyed by power. And not only killed but humiliated, degraded, tortured.

There is a phrase that describes the kind of existence that we as his disciples now face: it is "Saturday time," meaning not a day off from work, but the time after Jesus' death and before the astonishing event that will take place on Sunday, one that we cannot even begin to imagine. Saturday time is all we have, we think, forever: life without this person who seemed to transform our lives and the world. We are faced with a life of meaninglessness and despair. We in this church know all about this, for we can walk out of this building into Saturday time anytime we want. Most of us have probably done it. It is out there, waiting for us.

So we are present in the story as those who are driven by fear to kill Jesus. Yet we are present here also as those who love Jesus and are left by him, brokenhearted, stuck in Saturday time, not even able to imagine the great thing that is coming.

This double fact of our nature captures an essential and self-contradictory truth about us. We love Jesus, we kill Jesus; we call for his Crucifixion, his Crucifixion devastates us; we are guilty, and we are bereft. It will only be Easter, and all that it means, that can rescue us from these contradictions of our nature.

Today we are still in Saturday time. How are we to read and live with the story we have just heard? Are there in it, as it stands, any grounds for hope? Are there meanings in Jesus' death, even without Easter, that we as his friends and disciples can take away and live by?

I think so. For one thing, by this story we know for a fact that Jesus has shared the suffering that is an indelible characteristic of human life. He may have been defeated by it, but he has left us the knowledge that in our suffering we are not, or will not be, entirely alone. The ravages of disease, or the bone-shattering trauma of the loss of a loved one, or the lifelong damage inflicted by the abuse of a child, or the despair occasioned by depression, all these can now be seen as in some sense shared, not ours to face utterly alone. He has been there.

The fact that our suffering is shared in this way may also help us to accept—and not deny, as we so often do—the reality and necessity of our own suffering. The fact that it is shared may make that suffering more fully bearable, and enable us to be more conscious of it. This in turn may help us to become more compassionate, more ready to engage with the sufferings of others and more eager to relieve them. It may help us become more capable of that love in which lies our deepest fulfillment.

Even our recognition that we have a role in this story as the killers of Jesus, as Pilate and the mob, can be a good thing, for it may help us acknowledge our own need for forgiveness; this in turn may help us to forgive others, and thus to live less completely as prisoners of our own resentment.

Yet there is something in John's story beyond even these things, and of a wholly different order. For we are present in this story in still another way: not only as those who killed Jesus and as the friends of Jesus, but as Mary, his mother—to whom he says, *"Woman here is your son"*—and as the beloved disciple, to whom he says, *"Here is your mother."* Jesus gives these two people to each other in love. He creates a community of love, a community grounded upon the love these two have for him, and it will continue after his death. It is a way of building life in the face of death.

This is one of the moments in which Jesus is creating his Church, including ultimately this church, St. Andrew's, for we are a community of love founded on our love for him. We can trace our history back to this very moment.

What this means is that the larger Church, and our own church too—the Christian community dedicated to truth and love—might exist, and I hope it would exist, even without the wonderful Easter event that today lies over the horizon, unseen, not guessed at, wholly beyond our ken. It would be a bleak Church, a diminished Church, offering us at best a way of getting through life, not the utter transformation of everything that the Resurrection achieves and offers us. But there would be something very good in it.

What we have in this passage, then—in our own cruelty and irresponsibility as the crowd and as Pilate; in our broken-heartedness as the disciples;

in the love that is nonetheless possible, among the disciples, between them and Mary, and the other Mary, and among ourselves here today—is the foundation of possible lives, lives of love and truth and forgiveness.

This foundation is the gift of the text we read. It is undeniable. It is proven by our own feelings of sorrow and guilt and loss. It is not dependent upon the Resurrection. If we had nothing else it would be better than anything we had ever had. We would not have any idea what we were missing. Even Saturday time has by Jesus' life and death become a ground of life.

Today is Good Friday, the beginning of our time of loss and grief, so I can say no more except this: that the event that will take place to our astonishment tomorrow night, against our every rational expectation, will transform the world and our lives, and bring us joy and peace, beyond our imagining.

Amen

I suggest in this sermon that even without the Resurrection there might have been the Church, built upon who Jesus was and what he did—and built especially perhaps on what he said in speaking to Mary and John.

How would such a Church have been different from the one we have?

This is an important question, in part because there are many churchgoers who, while believing that Jesus had a special relation to God the Father—that he in some sense was God, or the Son of God—if pushed to it really do not believe in the Resurrection as an historical event. For them the Resurrection is an image, or a myth, a way of talking about the new life that Jesus' life and death make possible for us, not a literal truth.

What do such Christian people miss? Why is the Resurrection so utterly crucial to us? What is its amazing gift and meaning?

14

Sending Out the Twelve

In the passage that follows, Jesus sends his followers out into the world. They are no longer to stay with him, but to do his work on their own, in a world that may not be friendly, to put it mildly.

Here we have no difficulty locating ourselves in the story, for we too are sent, sent out to do the work of Christ. How do we understand our commission? How do we discharge it? What connection is there between what the followers were told to do and what we are to do?

The Gospel of Mark 6:7–13

He called the twelve and began to send them out two by two, and gave them authority over the unclean spirits. He ordered them to take nothing for their journey except a staff; no bread, no bag, no money in their belts; but to wear sandals and not to put on two tunics. He said to them, "Wherever you enter a house, stay there until you leave the place. If any place will not welcome you and they refuse to hear you, as you leave, shake off the dust that is on your feet as a testimony against them." So they went out and proclaimed that all should repent. They cast out many demons, and anointed with oil many who were sick and cured them.

The Church of the Mediator, July 16, 2006

May the words of my mouth and the meditations of my heart be always acceptable in thy sight, O Lord, my strength and my redeemer.

In today's Gospel, Jesus sends out his disciples, two by two, to go through the towns and villages of northern Israel, giving them authority over what he calls "unclean spirits." It is not quite clear exactly what these spirits are, but they certainly include the kind of spirits that Jesus had recently driven out of the suffering man into the Gadarene swine, which then ran over a cliff into the sea (Mark 5:11–13), and maybe they include all the mysterious ways people can suffer in their souls and bodies—like the woman we heard about two weeks ago who had experienced constant hemorrhages for ten years (Mark 5:25–34).

The disciples are to take nothing with them except a walking staff: no extra shirt, no bag, no money, no food of any kind. They are to ask for hospitality, and when they are accepted at a house to stay there as long as they are in the neighborhood. If any place does not accept them, they are to shake the dust from their feet as testimony against the place.

So: the disciples go forth; they preach that all should "repent"; they cast out many demons; and they cure many sick people by anointing them with oil.

For the disciples this is a crucial moment. So far they have been the followers of Jesus, watching him preach and heal. Now they are suddenly told, really without any warning, that they are to go off and do what they have seen Jesus do, but all by themselves. This is the moment at which they first act on their own—as of course they and their successors, including us, have had to do down to the present moment. This is in fact the beginning of the Church, the community of Christians that will survive the loss of Jesus, the Church of which we are a part here today in this room.

Imagine what it would be like to be those men on that day. Exactly what are they supposed to do when they visit these villages and towns? What are they supposed to say? Jesus is not very helpful here, telling them only that they have authority over unclean spirits, and that they are to take nothing with them and to shake the dust off their feet when they are rejected. The responsibility for figuring out exactly what to do, exactly what to say, is left to them.

These men must have been frightened by this responsibility, by their sense of their own inadequacy, by their nakedness and weakness.

What about us? Are we in this story too? Are we to imagine ourselves as disciples too, called to go forth and drive out "unclean spirits"? But if so, what can that mean? We may even say that we do not believe in unclean spirits. For us health is a matter of medicine, not mumbo jumbo.

But is that right? Are there not unclean spirits in our world that take possession of people, often enough including us? Think for example of the addictions that are so widespread in our society: addictions to alcohol; to gambling; to drugs of all sorts, both legal and illegal; to smoking; to impersonal sex; to TV games; or think of our obsession with money, or our anger and pride. These are unclean spirits, and we know them, or some of them, intimately.

Deeper than these specific addictions and diseases is something else, which Jesus I think would also call unclean, and in which we all participate to some degree: the selfish assumption that the point of life is for each of us to get, so far as we can, whatever it is that we happen to want. This is the premise of our consumer economy and the advertising business that drives it, stimulating an ever more intense and widespread hunger for material things—as if the mere gratification of our wishes and desires could make any of us happy and fulfilled.

But Jesus has told us otherwise. In the prayer he left for us we say "your will be done," not "our will be done"; and Jesus himself says, when he is about to be tortured and killed, *"not what I want, but what you want"* (Mark 14:36). To take our whims and desires and wishes and fancies as the proper guide to life, as to some extent we all do, is to live with an unclean spirit.

Or think of the sanitized and stupid way we sometimes talk about war—as though somehow we could participate in war, on either side, without inflicting hideous suffering on others and ourselves. Or think of the way in which we typically disregard the plight of the roughly 30 percent of the people in our own country, and many more in the rest of the world, that live in real poverty. The child climbing on a garbage heap for food in Lima; the child without medical care or without protection from an abusive adult in Chicago or Detroit or Berrien County, Michigan; the child starved of food in Africa or starved of love in Arizona; all these are

God's children, and our children too, and for us to live as if they were not—as we all do—is to live with an unclean spirit.

So I think we can indeed read this passage as speaking directly to us, telling us to go forth and battle the unclean spirits of our world, as disciples of Jesus in our own day. But how are we possibly to do this frightening thing, we may ask, especially when the unclean spirits are within us as well as in the world?

I don't think Jesus is telling us to strip down to one set of clothes and go off in our sandals, relying on the generosity and charity of the world, to cast out spirits. But perhaps he is telling us something not so very different: that we should try to change who we are—in the word constantly repeated in Mark's Gospel, to try to *repent*—and to be seen to do so. For it is important that we, like the original twelve, be visible disciples.

Part of Jesus' idea in commanding the disciples to carry no money or food or extra clothes, to depend on generosity of others, is that they are to be marked as different, not part of the ordinary run of life. Not priests or monks, for there was then no ordination, but something like that: people who are in some way set apart by their role. Others will look at them and say, "Here they come." So too with us: if we are to have authority over unclean spirits, maybe we have to become different, to ourselves and others.

I say this knowing all too well how little I achieve such a thing, but I do see it in other people and feel my own deficiency.

For there are some people—do you know any? there are some in this room—who really do seem different from most of us. These people have a way of being that somehow leads the men and women they meet, and the children too, to feel that they matter; to feel that they are accepted and cared for and loved; to feel that life and the world are basically good. They call upon the best in those they encounter, calling their goodness into life. They restore our souls. These people cast out unclean spirits by their very presence.

If they can do it, can we do it too? Maybe in fact each of us has done just a little bit of this, by a gesture of kindness or a word of comfort that has meant a lot to another person, even if at the time it meant nothing special to us. So the question becomes: Can we do this more deeply, more of the time, for more people?

Can we change who we are?

This is a daunting and frightening question, for we know we cannot achieve the change I speak of simply by force of will, or by application of mind, and we know that at best we can do it only imperfectly.

It would be nice in fact to evade this responsibility entirely. Can we distinguish ourselves from the disciples, and Jesus' commission to them, on the ground that they are all saints, while we suffer from the very unclean spirits we are meant to oppose? I don't think we can wiggle out of it that way: the disciples are deeply human and deeply flawed, as we learn, for example, at the time of Jesus' death, when every one of them either abandons or denies him. They are ordinary people, just like us in fact, with ordinary jobs and lives, until Jesus stuns them with a flash of light. Notice that in our Gospel passage Jesus does nothing to purify or perfect them—he does not bless them or anoint them with oil, for example, or give them a relic to take with them. He sends them just as they are. Likewise, he is sending us just as we are.

Can we say that he gave the disciples explicit authority over unclean spirits and that he has not done that for us? I don't think we can wiggle out of it that way either. We are his disciples, after all; we live in a world full of unclean spirits, some of which inhabit our own souls; if we are not to have the authority and power and duty to combat them, who will have it? I think here of the famous prayer of Saint Teresa: Jesus has no hands but ours, no eyes but ours. If we don't do it, no one will.

So we too are sent to oppose and resist the unclean spirits of the world: the spirits of addiction, and cruelty, and poverty, and lovelessness, and abuse, and brutality in all its forms. In our efforts to fulfill this commission we have only ourselves—our sandals and our staff—and each other to rely upon. As it was the task of the disciples to keep Jesus' spirit alive after he died, and rose, and ascended to heaven, so it is our task too. We are not excused from it by our own frailty, or by our own participation in the evil we are sent to resist.

But we are given something to help us: the support and love and forgiveness of the Holy Spirit, and of each other, as we struggle, always imperfectly, but with energy and sincerity, to build the community and the world Jesus has asked us to do.

Remember that Jesus sent the disciples two by two; perhaps we can go two by two as well.

Let us do it together.

Amen

There is a striking, even disturbing, gesture suggested in Jesus' instructions to the disciples: he tells them that, if they are rejected by the inhabitants of a town or village, they are to shake the dust off their feet as a testimony against them.

What is the meaning of this act? Is the idea that the townspeople will be excluded from the kingdom because they rejected the disciples? (All of the people of the town? How possibly?) Or is the excluding that takes place here not to be seen as punishment for a defect or wrong, but rather as the natural consequence of what they have chosen to do or not to do? That is, they have not turned towards the truth that is being offered them, and they must live without it. For the disciples to shake the dust off their feet would then be a kind of marker, an expression of the meaning of the choice the people have made. Perhaps it would even be an invitation to them, to rethink it, then or later.

But Jesus does not speak of dusting off the feet as a marker or an invitation, but as testimony against the people of the town, and the gesture itself seems to express contempt and hostility.

Why does Jesus tell his followers to do this? Do we ever shake the dust off our feet at others? Should we do so?

15

"To Whom Can We Go?"

In the passage from the Gospel of John that appears below, Jesus speaks in a way that his disciples find difficult and mysterious. In an earlier part of this speech, he has claimed to be the bread of life, saying, *"Unless you eat the flesh of the Son of Man and drink his blood you have no life in you. Those who eat my flesh and drink my blood have eternal life, and I will raise them up on the last day; for my flesh is true food and my blood is true drink."* What can this language possibly mean to his disciples (who of course as yet have no experience of the Eucharist)?

In what follows below we see that some of his followers find this way of talking impossibly obscure and threatening, and simply leave his company, apparently forever.

How about us? What can Jesus' statement mean to us? What sense can we make of it? What are we to do?

The Gospel of John 6:60–69

When many of his disciples heard [what he had been saying], they said, "This teaching is difficult; who can accept it?" But Jesus, being aware that his disciples were complaining about it, said to them, "Does this offend you? Then what if you were to see the Son of Man ascending to where he was before? It is the spirit that gives life; the flesh is useless. The words that I have spoken to you are spirit and life. But among you there are some who do not believe." For Jesus knew from the first who were the ones that did not believe, and who was the one that would betray him. And he said, "For this reason I have told you that no one can come to me unless it is granted by the Father."

Because of this many of his disciples turned back and no longer went about with him. So Jesus asked the twelve, "Do you also wish to go away? Simon Peter answered him, "Lord, to whom can we go? You have the words of eternal life. We have come to believe and know that you are the Holy One of God."

The Church of the Mediator, August 27, 2006

May the words of my mouth and the meditations of my heart be always acceptable in thy sight, O Lord, my strength and my redeemer.

IN TODAY'S READING, AS we shall see, Jesus is almost deliberately confusing or mystifying to his disciples. The question this fact presents to them is what they should do in the face of this confusion; to us it presents a similar question, namely, what we should do when we too are confused too—when we do not understand and cannot explain?

There is a real message for us here, I think, but to get at it requires some background. This will present its own difficulties, so let me ask you to bear with me.

Let us start with this. As we were told last week, in the early chapters of the Gospel of John, Jesus uses an image of *feeding* to describe what he is offering those who follow him. To the Samaritan woman at the well, for example, he says that those who drink from the water that he gives will never thirst again (John 4:14). Of course he is not talking about physical water—water from this special bottle or something like that—but using the image of water to talk about his gift of life to the spirit. Later he feeds the five thousand, this time giving them actual physical food, fish and bread—material food that is also meant to represent spiritual food (John 6:1–14). Then Jesus says, *"I am the living bread that came down from heaven. Whoever eats of this bread will live forever; and the bread I will give for the life of the world is my flesh"* (John 6:51).

Jesus is explicitly comparing the "bread" that he is with the manna from heaven that fed the people of Israel in the desert. ("Your ancestors ate the manna in the wilderness, and they died" (John 6:49). He is bread from heaven, like manna; but those who eat his "bread"—whatever he means by that—will live forever, unlike those who ate the manna, who were of course kept alive for a while by the food, but ultimately died ordinary deaths.

In his use of this image Jesus is making a claim that must have been shocking to his Jewish audience—and virtually all of his audience was Jewish—namely that he supersedes the great act of divine grace by which the God of Israel fed the chosen people when they were starving in the wilderness. Jesus is saying in effect that he offers more than Yahweh did; and, what is more, he makes plain that his gift is offered not just to the chosen people, but to all people—to whoever eats of the bread of life. This must have been very hard indeed for his audience to accept.

Then last week we read the following passage, which intensifies and transforms the image of feeding, and does so in a way that presents serious difficulties.

> So Jesus said to them, *"Very truly, I tell you, unless you eat the flesh of the Son of Man and drink his blood, you have no life in you. Those who eat my flesh and drink my blood have eternal life, and I will raise them up on the last day; for my flesh is true food and my blood is true drink. Those who eat my flesh and drink my blood abide in me, and I in them. Just as the living Father sent me, and I live because of the Father, so whoever eats me will live because of me. This is the bread that came down from heaven, not like that which your ancestors ate, and they died. But the one who eats this bread will live forever."* He said these things while he was teaching in the synagogue at Capernaum. (John 6:53–58)

Here Jesus' image of feeding shifts from the relatively innocuous water and bread to flesh and blood: he says *"unless you eat of the flesh of the Son of Man"*—by which he means himself—*"and drink his blood there is no life in you."* But if you do these things, he says that you will have eternal life.

What can he possibly mean by this language? To us the image of eating the body, and drinking the blood, is familiar, because it is the basis of the Eucharist. But Jesus' disciples had heard nothing of the Eucharist, and John makes no mention of it.

So what can this language of eating flesh and drinking blood possibly mean either to those to whom Jesus is speaking or to those who are reading this Gospel?

At last we get to the passage we heard today, which addresses that question, for it tells us that the disciples themselves could not make sense of what Jesus is saying. "Who can accept this teaching?" they asked.

This is a highly understandable response. For one thing it is not at all clear what Jesus can mean by this mysterious and cannibalistic talk about eating flesh and drinking blood. What is worse, drinking blood is expressly forbidden as unclean by the Jewish law, so even if Jesus is just using a figure of speech of some kind, it is deeply offensive. Finally, the very concept of eternal life is hard to grasp. Eternal life is not an Old Testament promise, and most Jewish people, then and now, have no belief in an afterlife. And—as everyone who has thought about this must have wondered at some time—what kind of life can *eternal* life be, when the only life we know is marked by constant change, by growth and decay?

So the disciples' confusion makes good sense. Yet when Jesus responds to their questions and doubts, he does not do so as the friendly and loving and helpful presence we sometimes imagine him to be. He does not clarify what he means, or try in any way to make it easier. In fact he makes it harder: "*Does this offend you? Then what if you were to see the Son of Man ascending to where he was before?*" This reference to the Ascension must be puzzling in the extreme.

Then, shifting his subject rapidly, he says: "*The words that I have spoken to you are spirit and life. But among you there are some who do not believe.*" This means, given what he has said, that some of his disciples will not have eternal life. Tough news indeed, and again puzzling in the extreme. Then he says: "*No one can come to me unless it is granted by the Father*"—suggesting that the Father is a kind of gatekeeper to salvation, determining who comes in and who is left out, with the result that we cannot on our own choose to believe. If that is true, does it mean that some of us are just doomed to death, others given the gift of eternal life? How can that possibly be just? This, too, is puzzling in the extreme.

Jesus is saying, in effect, both to the disciples and to us: "If you find what I say about eating flesh and drinking blood to be difficult, you had better get used to it; harder things to understand are coming, much harder." And indeed they are, especially the Crucifixion and the Resurrection.

So what are we, or the disciples, supposed to do with what Jesus has been telling us?

He has just identified a whole set of difficult issues—the meaning of eating the flesh and drinking the blood; the nature of eternal life; the mystery of the Ascension, which has not even taken place yet; the persistence of disbelief even among his friends; the possibility of predestination and hence of divine injustice—all of which have troubled the theologically minded for the past two thousand years and are still with us today. No one has solved any of them. Jesus dumps all this on his disciples, who are in no way prepared or equipped even to identify the issues, let alone think about them, and he dumps them on us too. For Jesus is surely speaking to us as well as to them.

These difficulties are in a real sense beyond the abilities both of his disciples and of us, certainly beyond our capacity for rational analysis. I know that I cannot explain, even to myself, the justice of God, eternal life, the nature of the Ascension, exactly what happens at the Eucharist, or what Jesus means when he says, "unless you eat the flesh of the Son of Man and drink his blood, you have no life in you." We are simply not going to be given the kind of clarity and certainty we desire.

This is perhaps the main thing that Jesus in this passage is trying to teach the disciples and us too, saying something like this:

> Of course you balk at what I have just said about eating the flesh and drinking the blood. But there will be much more to balk at before you are through. Life with me, and in my service, cannot be reduced to logical coherence, to human language, to human understanding. You will always live at the edge of understanding, in the presence of that which you cannot reduce to human terms.

Many of the disciples simply cannot take what Jesus is saying, and drift away from him. This is also understandable, for quitting is always possible, and tempting too. Maybe we have done it ourselves.

Those who do walk away are implicitly putting a question to the other disciples, and to us as well: "How can you do anything else, when what Jesus offers you is so strange, so illogical, so unprovable, and in some ways so shocking? Why do you not all walk out the door of mystery and confusion into the world of reason and sense?"

And why do we not? What are we able to say about how we have chosen to live?

Here, at long last, we get to the center of this passage, which is, as it so often is when he is present, the response of Peter. Peter does not seek to explain away all the difficulties that beset the others, nor does he tell them why they should stay. He does not claim to have understood what we cannot understand about eating the flesh, about eternal life, about the Ascension, or about divine justice. His response is completely different in kind. When Jesus asks the twelve whether they want to leave him too, Peter simply says, "Lord, to whom can we go?"

Peter sees that what is at stake is not a question of belief in the usual sense—the belief in the truth of propositions that cannot be proven, acquiescence in statements of doctrine, acceptance of one image or another of the spiritual life—but as something else entirely: commitment to a person and the life he makes possible. It is not that Peter can suddenly make sense of what Jesus is saying and explain it, even to his own satisfaction. It is that he needs and loves Jesus and the life that Jesus offers him, and cannot imagine giving him up. To whom can he go?

Now here is the point for us. This response is available to us too when we find ourselves in confusion and doubt, unable to explain to ourselves, or to another, either what Jesus has said, or what we believe, or what is for us the meaning of the sacred mystery in which we eat the body of Christ and drink his blood.

If we were asked by Jesus whether we wanted to leave him and go with the other disciples, with those who have quit, because like them we find what he says impossibly obscure or meaningless or shocking, we would probably have the impulse to try to explain it all, to make sense of it, at least to ourselves. But when those efforts fail, as they surely will, perhaps we can learn to say with Peter what we should have known to say at the outset: "Lord, to whom can we go? You have the words of eternal life. We have come to believe and know that you are the Holy One of God."

Amen

When Jesus says that no one can come to him unless it is granted by the Father, what does he mean?

Is the idea a kind of predestination, that you cannot exercise a choice to join Jesus, but can join him only if God has chosen you ahead of time for that privilege? This is a view that has had appeal to some great Christian thinkers, including Augustine and Calvin. But it is a hard doctrine: it removes from us the power of choice, and with that the responsibility for our choice, and with that the justice of any punishment for a bad choice or reward for a good one. It is certainly not consistent with the dominant view of our own day, which is that each individual is an autonomous, free, and responsible actor.

What then can be said for it? Here it might help to ask where your own faith comes from. Is this something you chose? Or was it a gift, an amazing gift of grace?

16

"Prepare the Way of the Lord"

Here we have the story of John the Baptist in the Gospel of Luke, which, like the other synoptic Gospels, draws a specific comparison between John, preaching in the desert and baptizing in the Jordan, and the prophet Isaiah. John is "preparing the way of the Lord," as Isaiah was too.

What can this language mean as applied to these two figures from the tradition? What can it mean as an exhortation to us, now?

The Gospel of Luke 3:1–6

In the fifteenth year of the reign of Emperor Tiberius, when Pontius Pilate was governor of Judea, and Herod was ruler of Galilee, and his brother Philip ruler of the region of Ituraea and Trachonitis, and Lysanias ruler of Abilene, during the high priesthood of Annas and Caiaphas, the word of God came to John son of Zechariah in the wilderness.

He went into all the region around the Jordan, proclaiming a baptism of repentance for the forgiveness of sins, as it is written in the book of the words of the prophet Isaiah, "The voice of one crying out in the wilderness: 'Prepare the way of the Lord, make his paths straight. Every valley shall be filled, and every mountain and hill shall be made low, and the crooked shall be made straight, and the rough ways made smooth; and all flesh shall see the salvation of God.'"

St. Andrew's Church, December 10, 2006

May the words of my mouth and the meditations of my heart be always acceptable in thy sight, O Lord, my strength and my redeemer.

The heart of the message we just heard in the Gospel of Luke is the call to "prepare the way of the Lord." The long quotation from Isaiah that contains this phrase dominates the passage and lives in the mind. This is a beautiful passage, magnificent, a kind of poem, almost an operatic aria, calling the people to prepare for the arrival of the Lord. Its beauty is a crucial part of its meaning.

What Isaiah and John both mean by "preparing the way" is of course the internal preparation of one's soul. For John the way to do this is by baptism and repentance, and, as he will soon go on to say, by adhering to certain basic principles of morality and righteousness: sharing your food and clothes with those who lack them, and, if you have official power, say as a soldier or tax collector, not using that power to abuse others.

The idea that the people to whom John was speaking by the Jordan in, say, the year 30, should be preparing for the arrival of the Holy One makes obvious good sense. After all, Jesus is about to burst onto the scene and transform everything. But, as you may have wondered, exactly what can this call mean to *us*?

We live two thousand years after the events described in the Gospel, and it may seem that we do not need the kind of prophecy John is making. We already know perfectly well what is going to happen: Jesus will emerge into public view, be baptized, engage in his own ministry in Israel, be tried and sentenced and executed on the cross, then rise again and be with his friends. Through the life of his Church he will be with us, even today.

From our point of view there may seem to be little point to the cry, "Prepare the way of the Lord." Our Lord came a long time ago and we know it.

We talk about Advent as a period of waiting and preparation: what exactly are we waiting and preparing for?

Here we get to the heart of the strange experience of living through what we call the Christian year. During the period between Advent and Easter our readings and liturgy retell the story of the life of Christ, always in pretty much the same way, year after year. The idea is that in some way we participate imaginatively in the story as we hear it: with waiting and anticipation in Advent, joyous wonder at the birth of Jesus, penitence during Lent, devastation on Good Friday, and the deepest joy of all at the affirmation of life and love expressed in Easter itself. We experience this story, that is, not just in linear time, once only, as it originally occurred, but in cyclical time, over and over. An important part of its meaning comes from the fact that it is so regularly repeated, so utterly well known.

This is all so familiar as to hardly bear saying, but for us in the twenty-first century it presents a real question: What kind of experience of waiting and preparing can we actually have, when we know the whole story all the time? Of course we can participate imaginatively in the familiar narrative; but is there for us any *real* suspense, any *real* waiting, any *real* preparation? Or is the Church here asking us to play a game of "let's pretend"?

I think it is not doing that. To explain why, let me go back to something I said a minute ago, namely, that we know perfectly well what is going to happen in the story.

Is that really true? In one sense of course it is, for we know the outline of the narrative of Jesus' life and death. But in another and deeper sense this story and its meaning are always beyond our grasp, always working in our lives in ways we cannot predict or understand. In fact we do not know, cannot know, exactly how Jesus will appear to us, or what his story will mean to us, this coming year, or the year after.

Partly this is because of the mysterious force of Jesus himself, which always eludes our easy comprehension. Will the Jesus we hear speaking to us be the baby surrounded by shepherds and angels; the prophet calling upon us to sell all that we have and give it to the poor; the healer and teacher; the suffering person on the cross; the amazing presence who appears with his friends in the upstairs room after his death?

Probably all of these things and many more. But we cannot fully grasp, once and for all, any one of these identities. Certainly we cannot put all them together. It is too much for the human mind to grasp. Although this life, this story, is in one sense familiar to us all, in another sense it is unknown, for we cannot get our minds around it—indeed we cannot get our minds confidently around even a part of it. Sometimes one fragment speaks to us, sometimes another, sometimes saying one thing, sometimes another. We do not know and understand it all.

This means that we do need to prepare to hear it. The story itself will be different this year. It is always full of new meaning.

The call made first by Isaiah and John and Luke, and now by the familiar season of Advent, to "prepare the way of the Lord" in our souls and lives is thus not a fiction or a pretense, but real. We do need to prepare our souls for what is coming, for what we cannot fully see or understand; we need to prepare for the presence and action of Jesus in our lives, for it is always fresh, always new.

But to say that presents the question: Exactly how are we to prepare ourselves? The baptism of repentance of which John speaks is not available to us, and we know from Jesus himself that conformity with conventional morality of the kind that John recommends—be generous, don't abuse others—is not enough. Jesus rejects the adequacy of this morality in the other Gospels, when he tells us that if someone asks for our coat, we are to give him our cloak as well (e.g., Matthew 5:40), or says to the rich young man that he should sell all he has and give the money to the poor (e.g., Mark 10:21). Jesus makes a much more severe demand upon us than John does.

So what are we to do?

I think this passage, without exactly saying so, is inviting us to learn and practice an art, the art of deep and transformative waiting and preparation—preparation for something expected but at best half understood, something perhaps at the deepest level unknown.

In waiting for Jesus to arrive we are, among other things, waiting for a baby, and surely many of us have some experience of that: as older siblings, as parents or uncles and aunts or just friends. We know something about what it is to wait for a child to arrive, and we know that it can be done well or badly. Sometimes we spend our time thinking mainly of other things—of our jobs, of the practical things that have to be done, perhaps of the pleasures and activities that the baby's arrival will make us give up—wasting our energies in a kind of fretful activity and evading the deep mystery that is upon us.

But sometimes we experience more fully our awareness of the baby in the womb, the presence of this person about to be born. We do not know who this person is, what attributes he or she may have—we may not even know the gender—but we already love this baby. We are poised in silence contemplating the unknown.

When we feel that way we become more conscious of our own deep hope for the child, and conscious of our fears and worries too. We become more aware of the fact that we are not in control of what is to happen or what it will mean. We can begin to perceive that we are in the presence of spiritual forces vastly greater than we are, a river of life with its own power and direction, which is about to create a new human life: a person who will have his or her own life story, his or her own relation to the world, his or her own experience of meaning.

We are in the presence of the creation of a new soul, with an eternal future. Our minds and words are simply unable to grasp and express what this means. The world itself is born anew with every birth.

Waiting for Jesus is perhaps a little like this. Our task is to learn to focus our attention not on superficial things but on what is most real: on the coming of Christ into our lives; on our incapacity fully to understand or control what we experience and imagine; on the miraculous blessing of life and the immense gift of redemption. This is hard to do, of course, and we all know how limited any success of our own must be, especially if we try to do it alone. It may seem daunting, to say the least.

But we are not alone. We have the Gospel and the psalms and the prophets; we have the season of Advent; we have Christmas itself; we have Lent and Easter; we have the sacraments; we have the life of our whole Church and community; we have a tradition and history that reaches back to Jesus himself, and to John, and Isaiah and Moses—and we have each other and the love we bear each other. We do not have to learn to wait, to prepare, all by ourselves. We experience a shared rhythm of life that calls upon us and blesses us—as this passage from Luke does, as our life together in this church does too. We are given what we need.

He is coming. It will happen. What it will mean we cannot know. We must wait and be ready.

Prepare the way of the Lord.

Amen

John the Baptist is in a remarkable situation, on a cusp between two worlds. He was raised in the culture of Judaism, with a rich tradition of texts and rites and roles, including the role that fits him, the role of the prophet. This religious culture offers a way of making sense of the past and the present, a way of imagining the future and living into it. This is part of who he is. He is formed by a tradition that renders the world coherent.

But he also knows that something new and tremendous is about to happen. Somewhere within him, below the level of language, is a perception, a feeling, maybe even a presence, which he must express but has no way of expressing directly. This inner experience tells him that there is someone about to emerge into view who is vastly greater than he is, greater even than he can imagine.

He has no adequate language in which to describe this person directly—this presence and force—but he finds a way to talk by invoking and using some of the material of his own religious culture. Thus he engages in the practice of baptism for the forgiveness of sins, which is a kind of cleansing ritual associated with repentance, and he invokes the beautiful and powerful language of Isaiah that looks forward to a future manifestation of the divine. But what is coming will be new, unimaginable, not what has been expected even by the part of the tradition that looked forward to a messiah.

John thus takes the language of his tradition and uses it to point to something beyond that tradition, inexpressible in its terms. The tradition gives him something old to say about something unutterably new.

Now think of our own situation. When we contemplate what we perceive of the reality of God, within ourselves or in the world—when we feel our own intimations of the presence of God within ourselves, when we see him at work in the creation, in the church, or in other people—we are situated like John, facing a divine reality we cannot really express.

We do have the formulas, and prayers, and rituals, and texts of our Church, and we can use them as a way of talking about the immediate reality that is beyond expression. But these materials of our tradition will not of themselves do what we want, in part because they can be used in empty and trite ways, as we all know from our own experience.

Can we, like John, find way to use, and to transform, the materials of our tradition—the old stories, the old texts, the elements of our liturgy, the formulas and prayers, the language made in the past—so that we can think and speak freshly, authentically, and responsibly about the deepest mystery in the universe and its connection with our own lives?

17

Jesus on the Beach

Like the story about Doubting Thomas, the passage from the Gospel of John that appears below tells us about Jesus' return to his disciples after his Resurrection. John presents Jesus on the shore of the Sea of Galilee, where he roasts fish for his disciples and eats with them. But Jesus says almost nothing to them beyond some directions to their fishing and the welcoming phrase, *"Come and have breakfast."*

What does this appearance mean to the disciples? Why does it take the form it does? What can it mean to us?

The Gospel of John 21:1–14

After these things Jesus showed himself again to the disciples by the Sea of Tiberias; and he showed himself in this way.

Gathered there together were Simon Peter, Thomas called the Twin, Nathanael of Cana in Galilee, the sons of Zebedee, and two others of his disciples. Simon Peter said to them, "I am going fishing." They said to him, "We will go with you." They went out and got into the boat, but that night they caught nothing.

Just after daybreak, Jesus stood on the beach; but the disciples did not know that it was Jesus. Jesus said to them, "Children, you have no fish, have you?" They answered him, "No." He said to them, "Cast the net to the right side of the boat, and you will find some."

So they cast it, and now they were not able to haul it in because there were so many fish. That disciple whom Jesus loved said to Peter, "It is the Lord!"

When Simon Peter heard that it was the Lord, he put on some clothes, for he was naked, and jumped into the sea. But the other disciples came in the boat, dragging the net full of fish, for they were not far from the land, only about a hundred yards off.

When they had gone ashore, they saw a charcoal fire there, with fish on it, and bread. Jesus said to them, "Bring some of the fish that you have just caught." So Simon Peter went aboard and hauled the net ashore, full of large fish, a hundred fifty-three of them; and though there were so many, the net was not torn.

Jesus said to them, "Come and have breakfast." Now none of the disciples dared to ask him, "Who are you?" because they knew it was the Lord. Jesus came and took the bread and gave it to them, and did the same with the fish. This was now the third time that Jesus appeared to the disciples after he was raised from the dead.

St. Andrew's Church, April 22, 2007

May the words of my mouth and the meditations of my heart be always acceptable in thy sight, O Lord, my strength and my redeemer.

DID YOU EVER WONDER what it would be like to be among Jesus' disciples just after his Crucifixion? At first of course we would have been crushed, utterly crushed. This man, unlike any other man, the man upon whom all our hopes were centered, was tortured to death like a common criminal. He died and was buried. Some of us saw his corpse, dead and gray.

But then, maybe, just maybe, in our despair we would remember something he had said about coming back from the dead. This would give us hope, perhaps; but hope of a very strange kind, since no one had ever done that before. What would the promised Resurrection actually be like? What is it we would be hoping for?

Perhaps we would believe that the Resurrection, if it happened, would be a triumph over death for all time, the greatest single event in human history, a promise of salvation for the whole human race. Perhaps we would also hope that it would erase our terrible experience of Jesus' murder, and confirm our deepest sense of his divine nature and identity.

So: wouldn't we expect his return to involve something like purple clouds, maybe with lightning flashing and thunder rolling, perhaps with angelic voices singing from the sky?

In fact of course Jesus does come back, but not at all as we might have imagined. In Jerusalem he comes to see his friends quietly in a locked upper room; in Galilee he comes to offer them bread and fish on the beach after a night's hard work of fruitless fishing.

This is both ordinary and extraordinary. As John tells it, the disciples have returned from Jerusalem to their homes and to their ways of life in Galilee. After witnessing the astounding events in Jerusalem, they are not out in the world spreading the Gospel, but have withdrawn, in puzzlement or fear, to the world they know. Jesus comes after them.

He has food for them, fish grilling on a charcoal fire—just as we might do—and bread. No one asks him who he is, and apparently they do not reveal that they know him. They just take part in the repast he offers them, bread and grilled fish.

This scene is full of charm and comfort, but it has its strangeness too. For example, neither Jesus nor the disciples say very much. The disciples do not even greet him by name. Why is that?

This surprised me at first, but then I thought: suppose someone we had known and loved deeply, and who had died, came back from death and was suddenly present beside us in the living room, say, or while we were walking on an empty beach. What would we feel? How would we behave? What would we say?

Would we talk about the deep issues of our relationship, reliving old blessings and old grievances? Or would we engage in a kind of bringing up-to-date about the children and grandchildren, and how the job is going? I am pretty sure we would not ask what life was like on the other side; that we would not gossip about family or friends; that we would not waste time deploring the quality of TV. This moment would be far too important for any of that.

How would we talk, then? Maybe not at all. Maybe we would sit in silence, overcome by pleasure and amazement at this embodiment of love, totally aware that words could not possibly speak to this occasion. Maybe we would just say, "Let's have a cup of tea." Perhaps we would just sit there, in silence, full of love and joy and forgiveness. It would be enough to be together soul to soul—all we would want in fact; maybe all we ever really want.

This is how Jesus is in this story. He is present, smiling I am sure, full of love; they share a meal; there is not much to say, just as there was not much to say in the upper room. As I imagine it, Jesus and disciples are just being together; what is present on each side is the center or core of the soul, the side that loves and knows love. This may look like nothing; but it is everything. It is soul present with soul.

But we know, as the disciples do not, that Jesus will go away again. What will that mean to the disciples, and what does it mean to us?

To start with the disciples, will they feel abandoned once more? "You have come back among us; why do you not stay with us?"

As I imagine it, this separation is deeply different for them from his death on the cross, and not just because it is in triumph rather than humiliation and defeat. Jesus has shown them not only that death can be conquered—whatever that may exactly prove to mean—but that he loves them so much that he wants, and is able, to come back to be with them, silently, presence with presence.

When he leaves them the second time, to join the Father, he leaves them with a charge or task: to build and spread his Church, the community of love that he has created. Now they can do it. They will not return to their old lives of fishing and net mending by the shores of Galilee but go forth into the world—Thomas all the way to India!—spreading his Church. It is as though he has given them a second life, by instilling something of himself within them.

Part of his gift to them no doubt has to do with a promise of life after death, but I think that is a rather small part: mainly it is the demonstration of love—the love that does not die when the person dies—and the realization of life of a new kind, here and now.

Now, how about us? What do Jesus' return to the disciples and final departure to heaven mean to us?

His departure to heaven means that unlike the disciples we never get to see the resurrected Jesus at all. It may be childish of me, but I cannot help asking: "Why does Jesus appear to the disciples and not to us—not to me?"

After all, if Jesus could appear to the disciples he could be present now, among us, at every stage of life: a glowing reminder that we are loved and guided, that each of us is supremely valuable, helping us to survive the dead places in our own lives and the sometimes terrible sufferings we experience.

Jesus could be with the tortured captives in Guantánamo or Egypt or Syria, not just in spirit, but in physical presence; he could be with abandoned and neglected children, and children whose whole lives are damaged beyond repair by sexual abuse; he could be with child prostitutes in Thailand or Michigan; he could be with the hungry, the sick, the homeless, the despairing, with those whose lives are destroyed by mental illness and depression, with those who are dying of loneliness—and all in an embodied way, a physical presence, with soul speaking to soul. But he is not.

While we are at it: not only could Jesus be present in the midst of those evils, he could eliminate them. Why did Jesus not make everything all right? If his idea was to save the world, why did he not save it? There is as much evil now as there was when he was born. What, then, is his Resurrection supposed to mean?

The fact is that Jesus did not change the fundamental conditions of human life I have just described, including dreadful suffering, systematic injustice and cruelty, heartlessness and thoughtlessness in all of us; including hideous murders like those that took place at Virginia Tech this week, or that take place constantly in Baghdad and Darfur and in every big city in the world.

Jesus did not come to change these things; he came to change us. That is the meaning of the Resurrection. He came to enable us to face the conditions of life, including our own stupidity and selfishness and carelessness, our own destructive emotions and thoughtless conduct, our own participation in evil.

Terrible things do happen in the world and will continue to do so. That will not stop. We should like it to but it won't.

Jesus came back not to eliminate evil but to give us the capacity to live out of hope in a world with a great deal of despair; to live out of faith in a world with a great deal of denial; to live out of love in a world with a great deal of hate.

What about his failure to appear to us physically, as he did to the disciples? In one sense of course it is true that he has not appeared to us in this way; but in another sense he has not abandoned us at all, but is present among us now.

He is present in the eyes of the suffering, calling upon us to relieve it; present where there is emptiness, calling upon us to make it full; present where there is despair, calling upon us to bring it hope. He is present as a call.

He is present in the life of the Church, especially in the Eucharist we are about to share, present in a way that is mysterious to us all but certain and real. He is present as the occasion for repentance, as the reality of forgiveness, as the creation of new life.

He is present in the Gospel, both as a voice of comfort to those who are suffering, and as a voice of correction to our selfish ways of thinking and living. He is present both as a comfort and as a rebuke.

He is present to us in the birth of new life wherever it occurs: in the season of spring, when the whole green world is born again out of its winter death; in the new baby, whose coming into the world transforms our sense of death and decay into one of life and hope; in every moment when suffering or pain or loss is converted into the ground for growth and life. He is present in the abundance of life.

He is present to us in fact whenever we are together in a moment of love, person to person and soul to soul, as tiny embodiments of his Church. This is true even, or maybe especially, when there is nothing grand or colorful about the moment, no lightning or clouds or heavenly voices, but just one person looking at another and saying something very simple and quiet, like "Come and have breakfast."

Amen

This is another story in which Peter exhibits his characteristic enthusiasm. When he recognizes Jesus from the boat, he leaps into the water, presumably to swim to him and get there as fast as possible.

But do you suppose that Peter actually could swim faster than the boat? Maybe so; but maybe his leaping into the water was not driven by the thought that this would get him there sooner, but simply by the immensity and intensity of his feeling, which required some immediate physical expression.

So his leaping into the water was a bit like a two year old racing around a house? Maybe so.

It was also Peter who hauled in the net full of fish, a hundred and fifty of them. At one level this is a mark of his physical strength and exuberance; at another level, more metaphorical in kind, it could be read as an image of his future role as a fisher of people.

Now let us think about ourselves: Do we throw ourselves into the water at the sight of Jesus? Are we exuberant haulers-in of fish (or of people)? What would it be like to do those things?

18

Sending the Seventy

This is a companion passage to one from the Gospel of Mark that we discussed in chapter 14. There Jesus sent out the twelve disciples, his closest friends and most reliable allies, to do his work. Here, by contrast, Luke tells the story of sending another, larger group, usually called simply "the seventy," of whom I think we know nothing beyond this story.[1]

I am including both passages and both sermons in this book, as a double reminder: that many of the passages have counterparts and parallels in other Gospels and that, perhaps to our surprise, even very similar or identical passages can, at different times, yield very different lines of response in the same reader.

In this passage, unlike the one in Mark, Jesus is sending his followers "to every town and place that he himself intended to go." Like John the Baptist, they are thus literally preparing the way of the Lord. Jesus also tells them to cure the sick and to announce the kingdom of God.

What would it have been like to be one of the original seventy? What would Jesus' commands have meant to us in that context?

Of course he is still sending out people, including us. What are his commands to us, and what do they mean?

---

1. Luke also has a brief account of the sending of the twelve, in Luke 9:1–6. A third version, combining elements of the Mark and Luke stories, can be found in Matthew 10:1–23.

Sending the Seventy

The Gospel of Luke 10:1–12, 16–20

After this the Lord appointed seventy others and sent them on ahead of him in pairs to every town and place where he himself intended to go.

He said to them, "The harvest is plentiful, but the laborers are few; therefore ask the Lord of the harvest to send out laborers into his harvest. Go on your way. See, I am sending you out like lambs into the midst of wolves. Carry no purse, no bag, no sandals; and greet no one on the road. Whatever house you enter, first say, 'Peace to this house!' And if anyone is there who shares in peace, your peace will rest on that person; but if not, it will return to you. Remain in the same house, eating and drinking whatever they provide, for the laborer deserves to be paid. Do not move about from house to house. Whenever you enter a town and its people welcome you, eat what is set before you; cure the sick who are there, and say to them, 'The kingdom of God has come near to you.'

"But whenever you enter a town and they do not welcome you, go out into its streets and say, 'Even the dust of your town that clings to our feet, we wipe off in protest against you. Yet know this: the kingdom of God has come near.' I tell you, on that day it will be more tolerable for Sodom than for that town. Whoever listens to you listens to me, and whoever rejects you rejects me, and whoever rejects me rejects the one who sent me."

The seventy returned with joy, saying, "Lord, in your name even the demons submit to us!" He said to them, "I watched Satan fall from heaven like a flash of lightning. See, I have given you authority to tread on snakes and scorpions, and over all the power of the enemy; and nothing will hurt you. Nevertheless, do not rejoice at this, that the spirits submit to you, but rejoice that your names are written in heaven."

THE CHURCH OF THE MEDIATOR, JULY 8, 2007

May the words of my mouth and the meditations of my heart be always acceptable in thy sight, O Lord, my strength and my redeemer.

In the Gospel reading today we were told about the seventy followers whom Jesus sent out to the surrounding villages. Jesus gave them rather complex directions as to how they were to conduct themselves—take nothing with you, wear no sandals, don't change houses, and so on—but a rather simple order as to what they were to do: to cure the sick and announce the kingdom of God. This they did, and then returned to him.

Jesus did not actually tell them how they were to cure the sick but we do know they succeeded. They came back to Jesus, full of excitement at what they were able to achieve, saying: "Lord, in your name even the demons submit to us."

In response Jesus says three things, and it is these to which I wish mainly to draw your attention:

1. *"I watched Satan fall from heaven like a flash of lightning."*
2. *"I have given you authority to tread on snakes and scorpions, and over all the power of the enemy; and nothing will hurt you."*
3. *"Do not rejoice at this, that the spirits submit to you, but rejoice that your names are written in heaven."*

Jesus' striking vision of Satan falling from heaven expresses, I think, his immense relief that the seventy could do what he asked. It shows him that it is not just Jesus and the twelve disciples who can spread the word and cure the sick, who can drive out demons, but that anyone, with Christ's commission, can do these things. All of us—the seventy in the story, the seventy of us in this room—have the power to spread the Word.

From Jesus' point of view, this means that idea of a Church that will live long after he ends his earthly life is a real possibility. Satan has fallen from heaven! From our point of view, it suggests that this story speaks directly to us, the present day members of his Church, telling us to carry on his mission. But exactly how are we to do what he asks? Are we to go barefoot from village to village? Are we supposed to cure the sick? How possibly?

The next thing that Jesus says is relevant to this anxiety. He tells the seventy that he has given them authority over snakes and scorpions and all the powers of the enemy, and nothing will hurt them. For them, this confirms their sense of wonder and amazement at what they were able to do. But for us it seems to mark a bright line of difference between us and them, for surely he has not given us powers of such a kind. They can cure the sick and we cannot.

But is that quite right? Are we positive that we cannot, sometimes at least, cure or mollify a disease, even a terrible one like cancer or heart disease or Parkinson's or ALS, by laying on hands and praying in the right way, to the right God? I don't think we can expect it to happen, but I am not sure it cannot happen.

If I look to my own behavior as evidence of what I actually believe, I certainly would want you to pray for me and members of my family in case of serious illness—as many of you have in fact done—and I would want to pray for you. We do this for each other. Of course it does not work one hundred percent of the time, as a magical cure-all. But that does not mean that there cannot be healing and curing through our hands and voices.

How about the power to drive out demons? Do we have that too? Think of some of the demons of our day: alcoholism; dependence on drugs; addiction to gambling; violence; sexual compulsions; abuse of children. And demons of another kind too, equally evil, those that eat at the human heart, telling us that we are worthless and no good, not entitled to be treated decently, not entitled to hope for goodness in life, or for love. These demons are everywhere. We cannot drive them out with a snap of the fingers, but can we be sure that we and our prayers can have no effect whatever upon them? I don't think so.

Again I think of the life of the Church, including this church, where I know that by prayer and love and patience demons are driven out, or at least their force greatly diminished—and demons of both kinds, those that make us hurt others and those that make us hurt ourselves.

However uncertain our powers may be, then, what this means is that like the seventy we are indeed called to cure the sick and drive out demons—by our prayers if not in some more direct way—and to proclaim that the kingdom of God has come near.

What I have said is I think true and significant, but the third thing that Jesus says seems to suggest that this talk about the powers we have, or do not have, is not the most important point. His concern is really not with power at all: *"Do not rejoice at this, that the spirits submit to you, but rejoice that your name is written in heaven."* Jesus is concerned with something deeper and more important than power, a question of the fundamental sense of self.

When the seventy came back they felt just as we would have done, full of astonished excitement at the fact that they could drive out demons. They were like the boy Superman discovering that he could fly, and full of the news. This was totally natural. Who would not have felt the same thing? You and I would have done so too.

But Jesus is telling them, and telling us, that this feeling is misplaced, a form of pride or self-centeredness: a putting of oneself in the place of God. For what they did was not really done by them, but by Jesus acting through them, and they should not claim it for their own.

Here Jesus is speaking directly to us. For it is common for us too to evaluate ourselves in terms of what we feel to be our powers. The high school football player who scores a touchdown, the college kid who gets a good score on his MCAT, the scientist who discovers a drug, the lawyer who wins a case, the business person who makes a lot of money, the political candidate who gets elected—all these people are pleased at the power that they have, a power that in their view does much to define them. We are all like this in our own ways, for we too desire power. In our culture we are largely defined by what we can do.

It is important to add that this skewed way of thinking works negatively as well as positively, and often with serious results. If I do not have the powers that in our world earn the esteem of others, and of myself, I am likely to think of myself as nothing at all, to fall into a kind of despair. If I am just a C student and can't play ball or get a date, what good am I?

So I think Jesus is speaking to us, as well as to his followers, and saying something like this:

> Don't think you are something special because of the powers you happen to have: because you are smart, or good-looking, or young, or healthy, or physically coordinated, for example, for these are all gifts from God. Don't think you amount to something special because you work hard and keep the law, for your power to do those things is also a gift from God. In fact, don't think you are something special because you are a loving spouse or parent or friend, or because you are generous to the poor, because the power to do these things is also a gift.
>
> The truth is that everything you think of as within your powers are gifts from God, not really yours at all.

What matters, literally the only thing that matters, Jesus tells the seventy, is not the fact that they have powers, but that their names are written in heaven. For this, he tells them, they may indeed rejoice.

This raises the disturbing question—the secret and alarming question that is perhaps at the heart of this passage: Whose name is written in heaven?

The names of the seventy are written in heaven, we know that: but of whom else can this be said?

Jesus does not answer this question here, but I am sure of this: that it is not only the seventy (who did his bidding); not only those who keep the law; not only the gifted and the lucky, the strong and the rich, or even the kind and the loving, whose names are written in heaven; but every single one of us, no matter how tortured by demons, no matter how ridden with sin—if only we can recognize it. From what is said repeatedly in the Gospels we certainly know that Jesus gives no respect at all to the claims of those who are powerful in human terms, and that the weak, the poor, the sinful all have a special place in his love.

Jesus is calling us to undergo a total revolution in the way we imagine ourselves and others. Power is nothing. Status is nothing. Money is nothing. In the language Paul uses in today's letter to the Galatians, "a new creation is everything" (Galatians 6:15).

I think that all of our names are written in heaven. But they are not written there because of anything we have done, or any powers we have. Rather, they are written in heaven because of what Jesus has done: in coming to live among us, in suffering death for our sake, in overcoming death, and all to save us all from our misplaced self-love.

This passage tells us that we do have a call, as I said before, including the call to cure the sick and cast out demons, which, if we can, we are to do and continue to do. But our deepest call, and that of the seventy, is actually much harder than that: it is to learn to give up our claims to power and what power brings us; to learn to rejoice, not in any power we may have, even the power to do God's work, but in the fact that our names are written in heaven; and then, hardest of all, to learn to live as befits one of whom that is true, with love and hope and faith and joy. And to live without fear: for what should we fear?

Our call is to learn to live as one of those who can turn from the natural human impulse to say, "I am so smart, so rich, so generous, so loving: I have such powers; I am something special"—and, equally important, from the impulse to say the opposite of these things: "I have no power, and am worthless: I am not special at all"—and learn to say instead: "All praise and thanks be unto you, my Lord and my salvation."

Let us, like Paul, learn to boast of nothing except the Cross of Christ Jesus.

Amen

We do not have the special powers that the seventy were given: to cure the sick (at least in the evident and dramatic way they did), and to tread on snakes and scorpions and all the powers of the enemy without being hurt.

How then does this passage speak to us, as people who are sent forth into the world? We can surely say "Peace to this house!" wherever we are welcomed. This gesture would seem a little odd in our world, but it might be a good idea to try it, at least if we could do so without seeming pretentious or self-righteous. (Would it help to practice saying it in different ways?)

Can we also say, "The kingdom of God has come near to you"? What would it mean if we were actually to say that to people we met, say, on an airplane or at a restaurant, or to friends when we were saying good-by after a pleasant dinner, or to casual acquaintances at the hardware store or on the beach? How would they take it? What would we say next?

If it just seems impossible to go around saying to people, "The kingdom of God has come near to you," we might ask ourselves: Is there some way we could use other words or gestures to say much the same thing, but more naturally and effectively? Or is the message Jesus is asking us to carry by its nature disturbing, uneasy, uncomfortable?

19

"Sell Your Possessions"

In the passage below Jesus is speaking to his followers, telling them to sell their possessions, to give alms, to make an unfailing treasure for themselves in heaven, where no thief comes near and no moth destroys. In this way they are to make themselves ready for the coming of the Son of Man.

There is an urgency here that probably made good sense to Jesus' original audience, who believed that something very big was going to happen very soon—maybe even the revelation of the Messiah who was to rescue Israel from the Romans. It was a little different for Luke's original audience, for they knew that Jesus did not offer that kind of militaristic salvation, but they did expect his Second Coming soon, maybe in their own lifetimes. In both cases the urgency is important because it would presumably make the idea of selling one's possessions more easily imaginable.

For us, two thousand years later, this sense of urgency has faded. We do not expect the Second Coming of Christ anytime soon. But we are still told to make ourselves ready for the Son of Man. To that end, we are told to sell our possessions and to give alms.

To focus for a moment on this last command, are we really supposed to sell our possessions? All of them? What happens if we find that we just cannot do it?

The Gospel of Luke 12:32–40

"Do not be afraid, little flock, for it is your Father's good pleasure to give you the kingdom. Sell your possessions, and give alms. Make purses for yourselves that do not wear out, an unfailing treasure in heaven, where no thief comes near and no moth destroys. For where your treasure is, there your heart will be also.

"Be dressed for action and have your lamps lit; be like those who are waiting for their master to return from the wedding banquet, so that they may open the door for him as soon as he comes and knocks. Blessed are those slaves whom the master finds alert when he comes; truly I tell you, he will fasten his belt and have them sit down to eat, and he will come and serve them. If he comes during the middle of the night, or near dawn, and finds them so, blessed are those slaves.

"But know this: if the owner of the house had known at what hour the thief was coming, he would not have let his house be broken into. You also must be ready, for the Son of Man is coming at an unexpected hour."

The Church of the Mediator, August 12, 2007

May the words of my mouth and the meditations of my heart be always acceptable in thy sight, O Lord, my strength and my redeemer.

Today's Gospel reading is drawn from a long section in Luke's Gospel that tells of Jesus' journey from Galilee to Jerusalem. It contains a series of Jesus' parables, his remarks to his followers, his interchanges with the Pharisees, and so on, many of which raise fundamental questions of economic justice.

Last Sunday, for example, we heard the story of the rich man who decided to build new barns and to stock them with his grain, then to take his ease—and eat, drink, and be merry. But God said to him, "You fool! This very night your life is being demanded of you" (Luke 12:20).

What Jesus says in today's Gospel is consistent with that story: *"Sell your possessions and give alms. Make purses for yourselves that do not wear out, an unfailing treasure in heaven, where no thief comes near and no moth destroys. For where your treasure is, there your heart will be also."* He then tells the disciples to be alert, always at the ready, waiting for God.

In these passages, and others like them, Jesus is calling for a total and barely imaginable transformation in our attitudes both towards material possessions and towards other people. He is calling upon us to be really different from the way we are. This demand is difficult to face—especially where the issue involves money, a topic that almost all of us find deeply embarrassing to think about, let alone talk about.

Jesus is not just telling us that money cannot bring happiness, though that certainly is true, or commanding us to give 10 or 20 or 30 percent of our income or property away. He is saying, give it all away. More than that: give up the whole idea of human life as founded on material resources. Cut all your ties to this part of what has defined you. Live a completely different way. He is calling for a total transformation of our inner selves, and our outer lives as well.

When I hear this I do not want to do it. It seems impossible. But I cannot rationalize away what Jesus is saying. If Jesus is clear about anything, he is clear about the danger of money and all that it means. But I cannot really do what Jesus wants; worse, I cannot even imagine it coherently.

Suppose I did sell everything I have and gave it to the poor? I mean everything, so all I had was one set of clothes, a pair of shoes, a coat, and maybe a dollar in my pocket. What would happen then? I might immediately start looking for work, to try to make enough to live on. But then I would have just reentered the economic system, the whole mentality, that Jesus is telling me to get away from. I would be acquiring and managing resources. Or I might become destitute and homeless myself, which would not help anyone. I would then just be an unhappy destitute person, feeling sorry for himself—and maybe feeling a kind of self-righteous pride at the same time for having been so generous.

What Jesus is calling for is not I think just the act of giving possessions away, but something deeper and in a way even more radical: an internal revolution—a revolution without which that act would not mean or accomplish very much.

What is this revolution? Someone once told me that Jesus is always trying to teach us to see things not as we usually see them—in our necessarily incomplete or twisted or false ways—but as they actually are, as God sees them. We typically think, for example, of the rich and powerful as important, the poor and weak as unimportant. But this is not how Jesus sees people. It is not how he wants us to see others or ourselves. Jesus asks us to see every human being as a child of God, of equal importance and value.

In fact, he is always on the side of the poor, the powerless, the marginal. For him the rich person, the person at the top of the heap, is in a special kind of moral danger, because he is likely to value his wealth and power far too much: to believe in it and to protect it, to feel superior to other human beings who do not have it, and to feel immune from the sufferings of life.

So Jesus tells us to sell our possessions and give alms to the poor. In doing so he articulates what is for me the most daunting practical challenge of the New Testament. In our world our possessions, our money, are extensions of ourselves. They are what we work for. How can we just give them up? Of course we can be generous and charitable, but that is not what Jesus is asking here. How can I divest myself of all I have?

But Jesus is right. Possessions and money do have an evil at their core, and the evil is that they draw a line between us. I claim what is mine, you claim what is yours. Think of the feelings of the child who finds a fifty-cent piece: it is his, not his brother's. We are like that too. In a deep sense we are what we have. Even in this church we think in this way: the new building we are constructing will be our building, not some other church's building. It will be paid for in part by the sale of an easement that we own, which is ours, not the property of some other church.

Money and property are in the nature of things scarce, and threatened by others, and we hold on tightly to what we have. They draw a line between us: on this side me and mine, on that side you and yours.

Jesus is telling us to erase the line between rich and poor, and, even more radically, the line between each of us and every other person in the world. This is what it would mean to give what we have to the poor. There is no other way to do it.

No wonder we are embarrassed by the topic of money. What it makes us feel is the very opposite of what Jesus preaches—selfish, cut off from others, anxious. My efforts to preserve what "belongs to me" close my eyes to those whom God also loves, who are in every sense my equal in importance, lots of whom have a tiny fraction of what I have—is it two billion people in the world who now live on less than a dollar a day? This cannot possibly be right.

Yet I do not want to give up all that I have. I want to protect against the possibility that I will be a crippling burden to my children as I get older. I want to have something with which to help them if they develop extraordinary needs. I want to be generous, but I want to continue to have the pleasures I now enjoy.

The Gospel thus leaves me, and maybe all of us, in an acutely uncomfortable position. Jesus is crystal clear about what should happen. There should be a complete internal revolution within us, producing an external revolution—a whole different world, in which all are equal, all share equally, in which there are no lines of selfishness between us. But this revolution is beyond what I can do, beyond even what I can imagine.

So I am left facing my own incapacity to live as our Savior lived and wants me to live. And this is true not only with respect to money. I love God, but not with my whole heart and mind and soul; I love my neighbors—some of them, some of the time—but I do not love all my neighbors as myself; I do not really love my enemies much, even if I try, and I don't always try; I have a hard time forgiving people; if you ask for my tunic I do not give you my cloak; if you slap my cheek I do not offer you the other one.

Jesus' disturbing injunction about possessions thus presents an even deeper issue that runs through the whole Gospel: we simply fail to live as Jesus would have us live. What Jesus asks of us we cannot do.

One term for what we are facing here is *original sin*.

I think the Gospel is teaching us here that a crucial part of what it means to be a Christian is to live with the painful knowledge of the fact of our own sin, our own necessary and repeated failure. This awareness is of course a distressing burden. But it is also surprisingly a gift, a gift of the Gospel, one of the gifts of Jesus' own life, for his story tells us that even though we now fail, and in some sense always will fail, we are always loved. Our own souls—damaged and limited and sinful as they are—share in the amazing world that Jesus is creating, the world not of scarcity and selfishness and hierarchy and fear, but of plenitude and equality and love.

For Jesus came into the world to save sinners. That means us. It is indeed good news.

If we can let both of these things live within us—both the recognition of sin and the awareness of love—then just maybe we can allow ourselves to turn to Jesus as we actually are, in the world as it actually is, ready in our hearts to confess our sinfulness as it actually is, when we say together, as we soon will, "We have not loved you with our whole heart; we have not loved our neighbor as ourselves." And maybe, like the servants in the second part of the Gospel reading, we can also be alert and ready in our hearts to greet the Lord when he arrives, in any of the many ways in which he does so, starting with the transforming and redeeming mystery of the Eucharist that we are about to share.

Amen

In this passage it is clear that the reason we are to sell our possessions is as a way of making ourselves ready for the Son of Man. I think the idea is that if we hold on to our possessions, we will be distracted from the real thing, the important thing, the coming of the Son of Man. But if we do sell our possessions we can be ready; and ready not only as Luke's first readers thought they should be ready, for the imminent return of Jesus to the world, but ready for something similar in our own lives, now, the manifestation of God in the events of our own daily lives: in the smile of a young child, perhaps, or in the warm eyes of an old woman looking upon that child with love, or in our own response the love these people share.

The life to which we are here called is one of constant alertness, an alertness that may be hobbled and disturbed by our other commitments. So Jesus tells us, *"Make purses for yourselves that do not wear out, an unfailing treasure in heaven, where no thief comes near and no moth destroys. For where your treasure is, there your heart will be also."* But Jesus does not tell us how to make these allegorical purses, just as he did not tell the twelve disciples how to go about curing the sick and driving out demons.

How are we to make purses that do not wear out, an unfailing treasure in heaven?

20

The Lost Sheep, the Lost Coin

Here we are told the famous parables about the lost sheep and the lost coin. They describe the familiar experience of losing something valuable, then finding it again and feeling great joy at having it back– greater joy in fact than if we had never lost it. We are told there is more joy in heaven over one sinner saved than ninety-nine people who are righteous all their lives.

This sounds lovely, but can it really be so simple? What does it mean?

Where are we in this story?

The Gospel of Luke 15:1–10

Now all the tax collectors and sinners were coming near to listen to him. And the Pharisees and the scribes were grumbling and saying, "This fellow welcomes sinners and eats with them." So he told them this parable:

"Which one of you, having a hundred sheep and losing one of them, does not leave the ninety-nine in the wilderness and go after the one that is lost until he finds it? When he has found it, he lays it on his shoulders and rejoices. And when he comes home, he calls together his friends and neighbors, saying to them, 'Rejoice with me, for I have found my sheep that was lost.' Just so, I tell you, there will be more joy in heaven over one sinner who repents than over ninety-nine righteous persons who need no repentance.

"Or what woman having ten silver coins, if she loses one of them, does not light a lamp, sweep the house, and search carefully until she finds it? When she has found it, she calls together her friends and neighbors, saying, 'Rejoice with me, for I have found the coin that I had lost.' Just so, I tell you, there is joy in the presence of the angels of God over one sinner who repents."

The Church of the Mediator, September 16, 2007

May the words of my mouth and the meditations of my heart be always acceptable in thy sight, O Lord, my strength and my redeemer.

THE PARABLES OF THE lost sheep and the lost coin we just heard are deeply comfortable and affirming, for they express God's infinite love for us and his eagerness to forgive us. The other readings are on much the same theme: Yahweh forgives his people for their betrayal of him (Exodus 32:1, 7–14); the psalmist asks for forgiveness (Psalm 51); and Paul describes himself as a sinner who has been forgiven (1 Timothy 1:12–17). All these texts work together to reassure us that we too can be forgiven.

Today I want to begin with this simple but remarkable fact: that in these stories our God is represented as a God of deep feeling. He is not simply a mechanical master of a mechanical universe, but a person with feelings—a God of joy. And he is a God of love too, for what gives him this joy is that someone he loves turns to him.

This is in a way obvious, but we often seem to forget it. For example, when people debate "the existence of God"—whether as students in high school or college, or in formal books of philosophy or theology, or in newspaper columns and book reviews—they are usually talking about a very different kind of God from the God we see here. They are talking about a God who is all-powerful and all-knowing, the governor of the universe, who issues commandments and wants them obeyed—not a God of deep feelings, of infinite love and joy.

I once read an article in which a philosophy professor said of himself, "I *hope* there is no God." What can he have meant? He cannot possibly have hoped that the universe is not governed by the active principle of love and forgiveness. He must have had that other God in mind, the totalitarian control freak who runs everything according to his iron will.

So in these parables, as in the events of his own life, Jesus is telling us that our God is a God of feelings, as well as will; that at the center of these feelings is love for his creation, including us; that his love for us makes him eager to forgive any one of us who will turn to him; and that when we do turn to him he is full of the deepest imaginable joy. Like the shepherd who brings home the lost sheep on his shoulders, he says to the world of heaven, *"Rejoice with me, for I have found my sheep which was lost."*

It is not only God who has feelings. We do too. Think about the intellectual debate about the existence of God that I just mentioned. We have probably all taken part in that conversation, but there is a sense in which it is irrelevant to our most important concerns. For our belief in God is in the end not a matter of intellectual persuasion; rather, it has its roots in our own feelings of longing and desire, of love and joy. Our belief is not the affirmation of a proposition we are logically persuaded to be true. It is an act of love. We should never be ashamed of that fact, for it is the center of life itself.

Here is a second point, which is more deeply connected to the first than may at first appear. In this passage the Pharisees accuse Jesus of spending his time with "publicans and sinners" (in the familiar language of the King James Bible). Who are they talking about? What does it mean to us that Jesus associates with them?

The publicans were tax collectors for the Roman Empire. They were not the equivalent of IRS accountants, but independent contractors or speculators. The Roman Empire, as an occupying military regime, sold them the power to compel the payment of taxes from farmers and merchants and workers. They were obliged to hand over to the empire a certain amount of what they extorted, but they could keep the rest as profit. If they were foreigners, they were despised by the Jews as a kind of invader; if they were Jews, they were despised as traitors. They are people it would be easy to hate, perhaps a little like Nazi collaborators in France in World War II.

As for the "sinners," I think that term was to the Pharisees as much a social as a moral term, mainly meant to define people whose very existence was an affront to solid citizens—people who were unclean, whose presence was polluting, who blatantly disregarded the requirements of religious law. The archetype is the prostitute: the woman who is outside of ordinary social protections, helpless, powerless, subject to systematic abuse, caught in a trap from which she cannot extricate herself.

It is not surprising that the Pharisees are shocked that Jesus hangs out with such people. We would be shocked, too.

What would comparable groups be today? Not so much the sinners we actually know, who, like us, are guilty of more or less socially acceptable offenses of pride and racism and dishonesty, or even people guilty of white-collar crimes like securities fraud and bribery and Ponzi schemes, but those whose very existence is felt to be an offense to "decent people": prostitutes and pimps; producers of pornographic movies, and actors in them; dealers in street drugs; petty thieves and burglars; maybe the homeless and publicly diseased, even if they have done nothing wrong. These people would be called, by some at least—and maybe by us some of the time—the dregs of society. It may be shameful, but almost no one we know wants anything to do with them. We would probably be shocked, just like the Pharisees, if our own beloved priest hung out with such people.

But—and here is the point and the scandal—Jesus loves these people, just as he loves us. He really loves them, all of them, and not just us Pharisees and Episcopalians. He knows how hard their lives are, how unlikely they are to be able to change, and he is telling us that there will be more joy in heaven when one of them turns to him than over ninety-nine good churchgoers like us. They are every bit as much the object of God's feelings as we are, and when they return to him they are the source of greater joy.

More joy? Does he really mean that? *Some* joy we can understand, but is God really *more* full of joy for them than he is for us, when we have tried so hard to be good all our lives? We have labored in the vineyard all day, they only for ten minutes, and they get more rejoicing than we do? "It is not fair!"

In fact it is not fair, and that is part of the point. Jesus has no interest in the kind of fairness that compares quantities and insists upon equality or proportion. He asks us instead to accept something very hard to imagine: that the love of God is not a scarce resource, but infinitely abundant, and that the joy he feels at the salvation of the flagrant sinner in no way takes away from the love he offers us.

This is true enough, we might respond, but in this passage it is Jesus who makes the comparison, saying that there will be more joy for the sinner than for the righteous person. So we still ask: Why *more* joy for them than for us?

Part of the answer is, as the parable says, that God thought they were lost, and they are found. He is a God of feeling, and he rejoices, just as we would, exuberantly. They have returned, like the prodigal son in the famous story, where the father is so overwhelmed with joy that he orders the fatted calf to be killed. When the good son, who has been with him always, complains, the father says, "Son, you are always with me, and all that I have is yours. But we had to celebrate and rejoice, because this brother of yours was dead and has come to life; he was lost and has been found" (Luke: 15:31–32).

So too here. Like the shepherd who has found his sheep or the woman who has found her coin, Jesus is calling us to share wholeheartedly in his joy, his exuberant joy, when someone who looks as though he cannot be saved is saved at last. This may be hard for us; but if we do not—if we cannot— share in that joy, perhaps we are even deeper sinners than we think.

Here is a third point. In the parable the shepherd and the woman simply find what they have lost—the coin or the sheep—and bring it home or put it on the table. But what Jesus does is different: he does not grab one of the sinners by the collar, toss him over his back, and haul him home saved. The sinner is not a sheep or a coin, but a person, with a will of his or her own, who must participate in his or her own salvation. The sinner must be willing to be found, and taken up. He or she must be willing to become the object of all this love and rejoicing. In theological terms, the sinner must repent.

To focus on the experience of the sinner may suggest another way of thinking about this story, one that undermines an essential assumption underlying everything I have so far said. Perhaps we have been simply wrong in assuming that we are more righteous, and hence a more proper object of joy, than the sinner who is saved. After all we cannot judge the quality of our own repentance, or that of another person. Our own repentance may be weak and feeble, the other person's heart-deep and strong, whatever his sins may have been.

It may be, that is, that there is more joy in heaven over the "sinner" who has returned than over the other person, the "righteous" one, not only because what was lost has been found, but also because the "sinner" has turned his heart more fully to God than the supposedly righteous person has done, more fully than we in fact have done.

Repentance may seem like a simple thing for God to ask of us, but our own experience is that it is not. It does not come easy, and sometimes it does not come at all. We know that we ourselves cannot always repent, and that we never repent perfectly.

There are many reasons for this, but the most important is the simplest and most disturbing: we love our sins. That is why we commit them. This is true of our tiny little dishonesties, our petty acts of selfishness or domination, our stupidest manifestations of pride, as well as our more serious sins, including those of which we may not even be aware.

But there is another side of us, one that would like to be free of our selfishness, that would like more than anything to accept the love and forgiveness God offers us, which we know in our hearts is our deepest hope and joy.

So we are conflicted. We resolve the conflict differently at different times. No one can say whether your repentance or mine is adequate, or just an empty and fraudulent gesture. Maybe the hopeless and despairing tears of a person who has really ruined his or her life are of greater value, a greater and more proper source of joy in heaven, than our pale and bloodless struggles with evil in a different form. We cannot know. But we do know that repentance is required of us; that we must turn our hearts towards the love and forgiveness that await us; and that this is often very hard or impossible to do. And we know that we are not to feel superior to any other person, ever, in the eyes of God.

In thinking of this story, we can put ourselves in the place of the ninety-nine righteous people. Then we can feel the unfairness of it all, and perhaps even take a kind of compensatory pleasure in our felt superiority to the repenting sinner.

Or we can put ourselves in the place of the sinner: the deeply inadequate and prideful soul who cannot save himself, who recognizes both his own need to repent and his inability to do it on his own. If we do that we will hear what Jesus is saying differently. We will not see our God as one who simply issues commands and insists upon obedience, certainly not as one who takes satisfaction in punishing sinners and rewarding the righteous, but as a God of feeling whose very essence is a forgiving love, a love miraculously extended to every single human being, no matter what he has done, a love so enormous that it moved him to the great self-sacrifice that has transformed the world: sending his son to live and die among us.

It is this love that makes God rejoice when we turn to him in our hearts, and, I should add, makes him feel sorrow when we do not turn to him. Our God is a God of deep feeling, not just of rational and moral calculation; and he asks us to live out of our feelings too—our own love and need and yearning, which is the true ground of our belief; and he asks us also to be ready to forgive and rejoice, just as he is.

In those moments when we are most aware of our own incapacity to save ourselves, we may find that we are full of amazement and gratitude that, in Paul's words, Christ Jesus came into the world to save sinners.

Amen

The heart of this passage turns out to be the attitude of superiority that we and the Pharisees have towards the "sinners," whether what is meant by that word is people who are in fact guilty of grievous sins or just people whose style of life is an affront to "decent people." The parable at first seems to invite us to accept the distinction between the "sinner" and the "righteous" person, but upon examination rejects it utterly. We discover that the greater joy in heaven when the "sinner" repents is justified both by the fact that the lost is found and because we, the "righteous," may well be greater sinners (and feebler repenters) than the "sinner."

What then are we to do? Never use a phrase like "the dregs of society" to begin with. Stop comparing ourselves favorably with others, especially in the eyes of God. And more even than those things, learn to ask: What does it mean that our God is not only a God of power and knowledge, but a God of deep feelings—including love, and joy, and sorrow? What would it mean if we allowed it to sink in, really sink in, that when we sin God himself is pained, and that when we return to him he is full of joy?

George Herbert has a beautiful poem on this subject, using as its text an injunction from Saint Paul, "Grieve not the Holy Spirit." The poem begins:

> *And art thou grieved, sweet and sacred Dove,*
>   *When I am sowre,*
>   *And crosse thy love?*
> *Grieved for me?*

21

The Pharisee and the Tax Collector

Here is another parable that involves a tax collector. Like the last one, upon which it could be said to build, it is highly uncomfortable for those who, like many of us, feel that we have done our best to lead the right sort of life, to be righteous and just and generous, observant in the prayers and active in the community. It is uncomfortable, that is, for people who are like the Pharisee in this story, which almost all of us are.

What can Jesus mean by the comparison he makes between the sinner and the Pharisee? Why is the sinner preferred? Where exactly are we in this story?

The Gospel of Luke 18:9–14

He also told this parable to some who trusted in themselves that they were righteous and regarded others with contempt:

"Two men went up to the temple to pray, one a Pharisee and the other a tax collector. The Pharisee, standing by himself, was praying thus, 'God, I thank you that I am not like other people: thieves, rogues, adulterers, or even like this tax collector. I fast twice a week; I give a tenth of all my income.'

"But the tax collector, standing far off, would not even look up to heaven, but was beating his breast and saying, 'God, be merciful to me, a sinner!'

"I tell you, this man went down to his home justified rather than the other; for all who exalt themselves will be humbled, but all who humble themselves will be exalted."

ST. ANDREW'S CHURCH, OCTOBER 28, 2007

May the words of my mouth and the meditations of my heart be always acceptable in thy sight, O Lord, my strength and my redeemer.

IN THE GOSPEL PASSAGE we just heard Jesus finds himself in company with some people who think that they are righteous and who are contemptuous of those they regard as unrighteous. Jesus sees this and tells them a parable about two people, each engaged in his own form of prayer.

The first is a rather stereotypical Pharisee, who says, "God, I thank you that I am not like other people: thieves, rogues, adulterers, or even like this tax collector." He goes on to say that he fasts twice a week, and gives a tenth of his income away, presumably to the temple or to the poor. He is righteous and sure of it.

This prayer is not attractive, to put it mildly. We are likely to see it as the expression of a misplaced and uncomprehending pride. But we might ask ourselves: How different is this prayer from what we ourselves actually do? Do we not sometimes thank God that we are not as others are?

Think about what happens when we give thanks for the blessings of our lives, say for our health (if it is good); for our capacity to maintain ourselves economically (if we have it); and for friends and family too (if we have those blessings). When we do give thanks in that way, is there not a danger that we will also be giving thanks that we are not like other people—those who are sick or friendless or poor? We do not say it; we would not say it; but do we not feel it, just a little?

In his story, "The Death of Ivan Ilyitch," Leo Tolstoy says that whenever someone hears of the actual or impending death of another, even a person he loves, there is a part of him that is deeply thankful that this bad thing is not happening to him. In this sense he gives thanks that he is not like this other person. This is not pretty, but it seems to be a part of being human.

In fact when we read or hear this story do we not find ourselves saying, "Thank you God, that I am not like this Pharisee"?

So here is the puzzle. It is surely right to give thanks to God for the blessings of this life. But how are we to give just and proper thanks for what we have been given without falling into the kind of self-satisfaction we see in the Pharisee? And, since our self-centeredness can affect any prayer—whether thanksgiving or petition or praise or intercession—we can put the question more generally and more bleakly: How are we to pray at all? For this parable shows that we can sin even when we are praying.

Jesus gives us a partial answer by providing another model of life and prayer, that of the tax collector—a despised figure in this culture—whose prayer consists of a single gesture, throwing himself on the mercy of God: "God, be merciful to me, a sinner!"

Exactly what is so different about his prayer? Let me suggest three things.

First, his prayer is an expression from the depths of his soul. It is not mechanical or routine, empty of feeling. He acknowledges his own sinfulness and his utter dependence upon the mercy of God. His prayer comes from his troubled heart. None of this is true of the Pharisee.

Second, he does not compare himself with others. The only persons present in his prayer are the tax collector himself and God. There is for him at that moment no one else in the world: "God, be merciful to me, a sinner!" By contrast, the Pharisee is engaged almost exclusively with comparing himself to others. He is thankful he is not like them.

The impulse to compare ourselves with others, which we see in the Pharisee and which we all share, leads naturally to many bad things: to pride, if the comparison makes us feel superior; or to envy and resentment, if it makes us feel inferior; or perhaps just to straight depression, if we think are in fact inferior. None of these is a good thing.

The person who regards himself as fortunate and prosperous is particularly likely to make the fatal error of thinking that he deserves whatever superiority he imagines he enjoys. Perhaps he even thinks that God values and loves him more than his supposed inferior. The fact that he is rich or smart or good-looking proves it. We do sometimes think this way.

But what the tax collector says is not comparative and it is not quantitative. It is not prideful or envious. For him both sin and mercy are absolutes, not to be quantified or compared.

This is wholly appropriate. When we stand before God we are in the presence of the Ultimate, the Absolute, the Incomparable; and what we should present to him is the core of our soul, which is also absolute. This is what the tax collector did.

The parable presents a third and more complex issue. As we read it, we are invited to think that the tax collector is suffering, both morally and socially, and knows it. Likewise we are to think that the Pharisee is prospering, both morally and socially, and knows it. This is in fact part of the basis of the Pharisee's sense of superiority. The superior do not suffer.

But as Jesus tells us plainly, the truth is the direct opposite of what the Pharisee thinks: it is the Pharisee who is truly suffering, without knowing it; the tax collector on the other hand, goes home "justified."

Here Jesus is speaking directly to us, because in our culture we assiduously try to avoid whatever we think of as suffering. We seek our own comfort and pleasure and happiness. We are satisfied and grateful when we have what we want: when we have money, and social support, and meaningful activities, and good friends.

But the parable makes clear that our capacity to judge the truth of our prosperity and felicity, and the opposite of these things, is often deeply flawed. Like the Pharisee, we think we know what is good for us. But in fact we are often quite wrong.

For example—have you ever done this?—let us engage in a thought experiment, and pretend for a moment that we could control events perfectly to fit with whatever we want. If we were in command in such a way, what would our lives be like? They would no doubt be comfortable, entertaining, pleasurable, without pain or suffering, without fear or anxiety, without loss. But this would in fact be an empty existence, a caricature of life, a kind of daydream, not a way of living on the conditions of existence we have in fact been given. If we could make our lives free of suffering and loss, they would not be lives at all, but a kind of death.

I once told a wise old friend that I wished I could protect my children from the (rather mild) suffering they were experiencing. She said, in her frank and determined way, speaking with a gentle but evident German accent, "Yes, of course, that is natural, my dear; but it is good that you cannot do that, for if you could you would deprive them of a full human life."

The problem is that the afflictions of life—the very things we pray to avoid, and give thanks for being spared—are essential to the full experience of our humanity, perhaps also to any experience of our God. Of course some sufferings can be unendurable, truly terrible, real torture, and it is hard to see how we could be grateful for them. But life without any afflictions would not be human life, and we should be grateful for at least some of them, in part because they may help us see that it is not our own will or pleasure or utility that does or should rule the world.

A friend of mine, a very successful and competitive lawyer, was blinded ten years ago in an accident. That affliction was terrible for him, as you can imagine, but it helped him grow into a different kind of person. He now says that, much as he would like to be able to see again, he would not trade what he has learned and become to have his vision restored. In a real sense his vision is better than it ever was. And think of the tax collector himself: his moral and social pain—his sense that things are really not all right at all—is the very thing that makes it possible for him to throw himself so genuinely on the mercy of God.

Jesus' parable is hard for us to live with because it explodes the whole idea, common in our era, that each of us is a separate unit, in control of our resources and in competition with everyone else for the goods of life. Jesus is telling us that we are not to look upon ourselves as winners or losers, even though our culture is constantly telling us to do that. We are, if we possibly can, to think of the afflictions of others as our own, the gifts of others as our own, for we are, or can be—such is the promise we are made—tied together by a web that makes your suffering and joy mine, my suffering and joy yours. This may sound extreme, and indeed it is, but it is also exactly what would happen if, as Jesus has told us to do, we truly loved our neighbor as ourselves.

Perhaps we can think of the Pharisee once more, and ask: What might he have felt and said about the tax collector, instead of what he did feel and say? That he loved him, that he admired his courage, that he respected his suffering, that he was his brother?

The truth is that we all end in weakness and death; we are all vulnerable to illness and poverty and loss; we all lose people we love and need. Such are the conditions of our life; they cannot be changed, and if they could it would not be good for us.

When we recognize this much, perhaps we can recognize as well that the suffering of each of us is God's suffering too, for Jesus has shared our suffering in its starkest form. To think once more about the problem with which we began, which is how to give prayers of thanksgiving, perhaps the parable is teaching us that it is this above all for which we can confidently and reliably give heartfelt thanks when we pray: for the love and presence of God among us.

Amen

One point of this passage is to tell us that all who exalt themselves shall be humbled, all who humble themselves shall be exalted. This formulation, like the others like it throughout the Gospels, seems to have a kind of contradiction built into it. If it is good to be humble—to love humility—isn't the idea that the humble will be rewarded with exaltation actually a promise of something bad? Likewise, if it is good to be humble, won't those who are exalted now, and humbled later, actually be getting a good deal not a bad one?

One way around this—not very good, either—is to say that it is actually never good to be humbled and low, but God offers you a choice: if you put up with being humbled in this life you will be exalted in the next, presumably free to crow over the now humbled proud man. An economist could explain it: eternal exaltation later is worth more to you than temporary humbleness now.

This is how the passage is sometimes read, I think, but it cannot be right. Jesus does not think in these ultimately self-interested terms, nor does he recommend that kind of thought to us.

Is it possible, instead, that the words "humble" and "exalted" have different meanings as they are used to describe the condition of people alive on earth and their souls after death? Perhaps to be "humble" in this life—truly humble not just humiliated—is a morally and spiritually good thing, for it brings you into contact with the truth of your situation and with the mercy of God. To be "exalted" in this life is to be like Dives, removed from the fact of human suffering, in oneself and others, full of self-pride and disconnected from truth and from God. But to be "exalted" in eternal life is not to be able to lord it over those who are worse off than you, but to live in the presence of God and his love. Likewise, to be "humble" in eternal life is not to share the state of spiritual truth that enables the tax collector to pray as he does, but to be humiliated in your own eyes as you realize how deeply you have wasted the chance of this life.

Does this work?

22

The Good Shepherd

One of our most common images of Jesus is as a shepherd. Perhaps most of us have seen Sunday school pictures of a tall man with long hair and soft brown eyes holding a lamb. Influenced by such representations, we are likely to think of shepherds (and Jesus) as gentle, sweet, and clean. But shepherds in the time of Jesus were a despised and marginal class. They were people whose job was to care for, and live with, animals. They were on the edge of human society. They cannot have been very clean.

For us the image is highly sentimentalized, partly because most of us do not know any shepherds, partly because we so often use the image of the shepherd in thinking both of bishops—with their shepherd crooks—and of pastors, who carry the Latin name for *shepherd* in their title.

What does the image of the shepherd mean for Jesus? Why does he use it as he does?

Where are we in this story?

The Gospel of John 10:1–10

"Very truly, I tell you, anyone who does not enter the sheepfold by the gate but climbs in by another way is a thief and a bandit. The one who enters by the gate is the shepherd of the sheep. The gatekeeper opens the gate for him, and the sheep hear his voice.

He calls his own sheep by name and leads them out. When he has brought out all his own, he goes ahead of them, and the sheep follow him because they know his voice. They will not follow a stranger, but they will run from him because they do not know the voice of strangers."

Jesus used this figure of speech with them, but they did not understand what he was saying to them. So again Jesus said to them, "Very truly, I tell you, I am the gate for the sheep. All who came before me are thieves and bandits; but the sheep did not listen to them. I am the gate. Whoever enters by me will be saved, and will come in and go out and find pasture. The thief comes only to steal and kill and destroy. I came that they may have life, and have it abundantly.

"I am the good shepherd. The good shepherd lays down his life for the sheep. The hired hand, who is not the shepherd and does not own the sheep, sees the wolf coming and leaves the sheep and runs away—and the wolf snatches them and scatters them. The hired hand runs away because a hired hand does not care for the sheep.

"I am the good shepherd. I know my own and my own know me, just as the Father knows me and I know the Father. And I lay down my life for the sheep. I have other sheep that do not belong to this fold. I must bring them also, and they will listen to my voice. So there will be one flock, one shepherd. For this reason the Father loves me, because I lay down my life in order to take it up again. No one takes it from me, but I lay it down of my own accord. I have power to lay it down, and I have power to take it up again. I have received this command from my Father."

St. Andrew's Church, April 13, 2008

May the words of my mouth and the meditations of my heart be always acceptable in thy sight, O Lord, my strength and my redeemer.

In the passage we just heard, Jesus uses the image of shepherd and sheepfold to describe himself and his relation to his followers. This is certainly a familiar way to talk, but I think there is something a bit strange here as well.

What most strikes me as odd is Jesus' central statement that as the good shepherd he will lay down his life for his sheep.

Of course I know that this is meant as an image of selfless love, and that he is really talking about his Crucifixion for our sake. But I cannot help thinking, perhaps in too literal-minded a way, about the sheep. What happens to them when the shepherd dies? What kind of shepherd is Jesus actually proposing to be?

The problem is that if a real shepherd dies, his sheep will be without any protection, utterly exposed to the thieves and bandits and wolves of which Jesus speaks. I think that if we were to go to shepherding school we would be told that it is much better that one or two sheep should be killed than that the shepherd himself should die, leaving them all at the mercy of the enemy. That seems obvious.

The question all this presents—"What will happen to the sheep when the shepherd has died for them?"—is a real one not only for the sheep, as I imagine them, but for the disciples too, though they do not quite know it yet. What are they to do when Jesus has died? This prospect must be frightening to them. It is a question for us too, as his disciples two thousand years later.

Where does his death leave us, as the sheep for whom he has died? Who is to care for us? Where is our shepherd, our sheepfold?

Of course we know that Jesus comes back on Easter, and in this way demonstrates his victory over death, a victory on which we have built our Church and our lives. But we should still ask what this victory means.

It does not mean that Jesus will remain on earth to the end, protecting his sheep. We know that he will leave his disciples when he ascends to heaven, and that he will leave us too. Nor does it mean that we shall be spared the experience of death. We shall suffer pain, and loss, sometimes beyond our capacity to endure it. We shall in the usual sense die.

Jesus' death for us does mean, as we are told by him and by others, that we shall have an eternal life after death. But this is a most difficult idea to grasp. In some way it is deeply mysterious, beyond our present knowledge.

This makes me want to ask: Is there another sense in which Jesus achieves a victory over death, one that we can experience directly and immediately?

So let us think for a minute about death. We know that we shall die, as all organic creatures do; but we also know that this kind of death is an inherent part of the life we have been given. Death is not in itself an evil. It is a necessity; in real sense it is also a good thing, necessary to the continuation of life itself.

For life as we know it involves a process of constant renewal, the making of new life. Of this process death is an essential part. We must die to make room for others, as our earlier selves must die to make room for the growth of our present selves. When I watched my daughter being born, years ago, turning from blue to pink as she drew her first breath, I suddenly thought of my mother, who had died fifteen years earlier. I realized that I could now see her death in an entirely new light: not just as a painful and enduring loss, which it surely was, but as making possible this new and wonderful life before me and the love this life called forth.

So what is the evil of death? From what do we so deeply want to be saved?

Part of it—a big part—is that it so often comes at the wrong time and in the wrong way to the wrong people. If a very old and frail person dies painlessly in his or her sleep, we think that not an evil but a blessing. We would presumably think that in our own case.

What *is* evil is that death comes with suffering; that it comes to children; that it comes to us when we are not ready for it. "Not today," we say, "not this way"; but it happens—in car crashes, or by disease, or by violence. Death is often random and unfair, untimely and pointless.

Of course it would be terrible to have to say good-bye to life, and to the people we love, before our time, but I wonder if the very worst thing about death is not anything I have mentioned but something else: the way it works away at our minds, like a kind cancer, claiming that our life has no meaning. Death can strike any of us at random, without justice or sense. It can fall upon the wholly innocent. Any one of us can be killed in an auto crash, or contract terminal cancer, or lose our bodily control or our very minds. When any of those things happens, there is a voice in us that says, "See: What did I tell you? Life has no meaning after all. It is just growing and breeding and dying, in an endless and meaningless cycle. There is no good, no evil; nothing really matters. The story of life is the momentary survival of the strongest and the luckiest. But death rules in the end."

This is the devil speaking; and what makes his voice echo so loudly in our minds is our own fear that it is true. It is an expression of the great principle of No Meaning. It is true that when death comes to us we may discover that nothing upon which we have founded our lives has after all any real value: certainly not money, or power, or reputation, or prestige. All these fade into nothing, and death's cry of "No Meaning" resonates through our being. We seem to have nothing with which to face the facts of suffering and death and their claim of meaninglessness.

This is the point at which Jesus speaks to us. He tells us that if we live in the light of his love, we shall have abundant life—true life, not the kind of death-in-life that we and others have so often experienced. Our every act of love, given or received, our every moment of selfless concern for another, is a participation in divine love, in a life that can never end. Every day lived in love with others, every gesture of love, has a significance that can never die. We know this because we know that when we face death we shall never find ourselves saying that the love we gave or received or shared was meaningless. As Jesus teaches us, love is the ground of meaning and of life. It is the only ground.

In our Gospel passage Jesus uses the image of the shepherd to tell us something about the kind of love he offers us and how it has such power.

First, he tells us that, as our shepherd, he knows us all by name. He knows each of us. He is the shepherd not just of a flock, but of each sheep in the flock. This is new. The God of the Old Testament was mainly the God of a nation, a whole people. Our God, Jesus is saying, is not the God of a nation, but a God for every single person. To him every one of us is real. We exist for him as individual persons, every one of us. We can pray to him in our own names.

For Jesus each human soul is of infinite value. He will never sacrifice one of us for the supposed good of the whole—as Caiaphas will recommend that Jesus himself be sacrificed for the good of the people (John 11:50). The only sacrifice that Jesus recognizes is the one he himself will make, on behalf of all of us, the sacrifice that will end all sacrifices.

This image of total giving is not what one would learn in shepherding school. It is not what we would call cost justified. It is certainly not an image of life as survival of the fittest. But what Jesus says and does, here and elsewhere, is never meant to be cost justified. He transforms the image of the shepherd, indeed any image of human life, to mark out wholly new possibilities, not dreamt of in our philosophy.

He also tells us that his sheep know his voice. I think this is true of sheep. They do not see well, but can hear each other's cries and the calls of the shepherd. For them the shepherd is his voice. Think of our own experience: we have not seen Jesus, but we have all heard him. We have heard his Word, as we did when we heard the Gospel read this morning in this very church, and it is his words we are thinking about right now. We are hearing Jesus' voice, hearing his voice that does not die, and he is telling us that he knows us by name and loves each of us with an unbounded love.

When our shepherd dies for us he does not leave us abandoned or orphaned, but returns to us, remains with us.

Finally, Jesus says that the good shepherd leads his sheep to the sheepfold. Where is our sheepfold? The sheepfold to which Jesus leads us is right here, in this church—in other churches, in any community of Christian faith: in the love and care and respect we have for each other, and for the world. It is here that we can most completely face the true conditions of our lives, including the uncertainty, pain, death, and grief that are an inherent part of our life.

Here our deaths are recognized and mourned; here our baptisms take place, honoring the births that our deaths make possible; here our weddings happen, too, the weddings that lead to new life; and here we participate in the Eucharist, which binds it all together.

Here death is in a most direct and immediate sense faced and conquered. For here we are shown that we do not need to be afraid of death; we need not fear its claim that life has no meaning.

Amen

In the Gospel passage we read above Jesus says, "I have other sheep who do not belong to this fold." What can he mean by that?

One possibility, and perhaps the standard reading of this text, is to say that Jesus means to include Gentiles as well as Jews in the

Church he is establishing. This would support the stance later taken by Paul that Christ erases the distinctions created by history and society—distinctions between Gentile and Jew, man and woman, slave and free. The promise of Jesus is available to all people who turn to him. This is an immensely appealing position and it is consistent with much of what Jesus says in the Gospels. It is also clear that the early Church took this position and never looked back.

But there is another reading, perhaps fanciful, but let me say it: Jesus is rejecting the claims of any one division of his Church to be the sole and exclusive authority—to be in effect the only true Church.

It is almost as though he is envisaging what has occurred, namely that his Church has divided, and divided again, in many ways, on many grounds. The various parts of this Church differ in theology and liturgical practice and ecclesiastical structure, among other things. Is one right and the others simply wrong? That is the standard view that pretty much each branch of the Church has taken, but I think Jesus is here saying it *is* wrong: He has sheep that do not belong to this fold, or that fold, or this other one either.

On this view the right way to think about the Church is that it includes all the Christian churches, with all their differences in theory and practice. No church is more than one branch or unit of the larger Church, the universal Church.

Could we go even farther, and say that Jesus is thinking here of those who do not know him and his Church at all—people in India who think of themselves as Hindus, or Persians or Arabs who think of themselves as Muslims, or Japanese who think of themselves as Buddhists, or animists who see the power and beauty of God in the natural world—in the tree, or fountain, or lake, or garden? Jesus would be saying that all people are his sheep, the object of his love and care.

Can this be wrong?

23

"You in Me, and I in You"

This is another part of the long speech, found in the Gospel of John, that Jesus gave to his disciples just before his death. As we saw in chapter one, where we read another part of it, the speech is highly repetitive, and some people find it too wordy, too long. But it is possible to love it deeply, in part for its special style, which is musical, almost liturgical in quality. (As you read it, you might ask which group you belong to.)

In this part of the speech Jesus talks about the Holy Spirit who will come to his friends as an Advocate, after he has left them. Jesus does not explain exactly what the Advocate will do; he certainly does not articulate the doctrine of the Trinity, though we can see it emerging, as the Holy Spirit comes to be added to the Father and the Son.

Who is this Advocate, this Holy Spirit, for Jesus, in this speech? Who is this Holy Spirit for us?

The Gospel of John 14:15–21

"If you love me, you will keep my commandments. And I will ask the Father, and he will give you another Advocate, to be with you forever. This is the Spirit of truth, whom the world cannot receive, because it neither sees him nor knows him. You know him, because he abides with you, and he will be in you.

"I will not leave you orphaned; I am coming to you. In a little while the world will no longer see me, but you will see me; because I live, you also will live. On that day you will know that I am in my Father, and you in me, and I in you. They who have my commandments and keep them are those who love me; and those who love me will be loved by my Father, and I will love them and reveal myself to them."

The Church of the Mediator, April 27, 2008

May the words of my mouth and the meditations of my heart be always acceptable in thy sight, O Lord, my strength and my redeemer.

The passage from the Gospel of John we heard today is the second part of Jesus' long speech of farewell to his disciples, given to them on the night before he died. You may remember that last week's reading included the first part of the speech, in which Jesus said that he was leaving the disciples to prepare a place for them, in his Father's house of "many mansions" (John 14:12).

Today Jesus goes on to tell his disciples—and us—that he will ask the Father to send us an Advocate, the Spirit of Truth, whom the world will not see or know, but whom we shall know because he will be in us: "*You will know that I am in my Father, and you in me, and I in you. They who have my commandments and keep them are those who love me; and those who love me will be loved by my Father, and I will love them and reveal myself to them.*"

I think this passage, and the whole speech of which it is a part, is incredibly beautiful. Once I start reading these words, even to myself, I just want to hear them again, as Jesus says them, repeated with slight variations in detail but always with the deepest and strongest and simplest theme: the love of God for us, of us for God. They are hypnotic, a bit like a piece of Bach's harpsichord music. They fill the mind. The beauty and trancelike quality of these words are in fact important parts of their meaning, for we, like the disciples, feel reassured and loved by the words themselves, held by the sentences and by the sound a bit as a child is held in his or her parent's arms.

But what Jesus is saying also has significance of a more explicitly theological kind. Though we may not be aware of it, in this passage John explicates, indeed he may actually discover, what is perhaps the deepest mystery of the Christian faith, the doctrine of the Trinity: that is, the awareness that there is a deep identity between the Father and the Son, and between each of them and the Holy Spirit; yet that there are important differences among them too. They are somehow the same, but different too.

I don't know if you have ever tried to explain or defend this doctrine to a questioner or doubter, or even to yourself, but it is difficult in the extreme. Historically the church has found it pretty much impossible as well, actually dividing or splitting, several times, over exactly what the Trinity is.

Of course I cannot fully explain it either, but I think today's Gospel may give some insight into how this idea of God arose and some sense of what its content might be.

We can start with Jesus. Some people want to say that he was a uniquely great ethical teacher, but only a human being, not a God. But for us Christians it is simply not enough that he be just a good person, like Gandhi or Martin Luther King, say. If the gap that exists between a loving Creator and his fallen creation is ever to be closed, it must be by God's action, not ours. For us, Jesus is that action; Jesus is God coming to share our humanity, our embodied nature, our suffering. He is the presence of God among us. So for us it makes total sense both that Jesus and the Father share a fundamental identity, and that they have different roles.

How about the Holy Spirit? In the story that John is telling, Jesus is at the point where he will die for us, and leave us, when he is crucified. He will of course return at the Resurrection, but, as he knows, he will then leave his disciples once more, when he ascends to heaven. What then? If he just goes back to heaven, leaving everything as it is, what will he have achieved? What will have changed?

You can see that we really need something here, that the story itself needs something, and it is that something which Jesus offers us in this passage: the promise of another aspect or embodiment or form of God, the one called the Spirit, the Comforter, or the Advocate.

The Spirit will be the presence of God among us when Jesus has gone.

It is impossible for us to explain the exact relation between Father, Son, and Spirit: Has the Son existed forever, or did he come into existence when he was begotten? Is the Spirit coming into existence now, as Jesus might seem to say, or has the Spirit been there all along, in fact since the creation of the world in Genesis? Does the Spirit proceed from the Father or from the Father and the Son? These issues have divided Christians into opposing camps for centuries.

But Jesus' speech is not theoretical in nature, and does not really ask us to think about such questions. Rather, the heart of this speech is the active and tangible presence of Jesus' love, with its movement and energy expressing the promise of the Spirit. This is I think why the musical beauty of the passage—which is present in the Greek as well as the English—is so important. It makes us feel the quality of this love—not just as an idea, but as a reality, a living force, reaching over two thousand years to touch our hearts. When we hear it, we know and we believe.

Jesus' speech presents a second, related issue, having to do with what for lack of a better term might be called the "insideness" of God. In the course of this speech Jesus tells us that the Father is in Jesus, that Jesus is in the Father, that Jesus is in us, that we are in Jesus, that the Spirit is in us. Jesus is talking about a God who lives not only in each of his three established forms, but in us as well. "The Spirit it is not out there," Jesus is in effect saying, "the Spirit is in you and in me." And Jesus is not out there; he is in you and in me.

This is something new, a profound transformation of the tradition of the Old Testament, in which God is always separate from human beings. In the Old Testament he is sometimes on earth, his word comes to people and transforms them, he inspires his prophets, he wrestles with Jacob, he speaks to Moses, but he is not seen to be permanently within any of us, alive within us. What Jesus says is thus utterly new and amazing: that God is not just "with us"—the meaning of the Hebrew word *Emmanuel*—he is within us.

The idea that God is within us changes everything. We no longer have to assimilate God from outside by learning to understand complex theological principles (like the Trinity); or by engaging in a chain of reasoning that will satisfy us that in fact God exists, and tell us who he is; or by trying without success to make our broken selves more perfect and therefore acceptable; or by conforming our behavior to strictures we do not understand; or by acquiescing in an authoritarian ecclesiastical or intellectual structure; or by losing ourselves in a sea of sentimental religious feeling, constantly affirming what we do not and cannot really believe.

We do not have to do those things because God is within us, within each one of us: as the voice that tells us what is right and wrong, as the principle of love, as the knowledge that a world of human inequality is unjust, and as the constant reminder that our self-determined goals and satisfactions are all too often only dust and ashes.

This is what Jesus is saying, and it is wonderful, wonderful beyond our comprehension: God is within us.

But this understanding has its own dangers. For how am I to know whether this or that impulse or feeling or insight or direction to conduct comes from the God within me, or from the Me within me? Carried to its extreme, the recognition that God is within each one of us could lead to the end of the Church, of the very community Jesus sought to establish. For each of us would be his or her own Gospel interpreter, even his or her own Gospel writer; each of us would be relying in an unchecked way on what might be nothing but a selfish or grandiose or deluded or actually crazy aspect of the self.

In the passage given above, Jesus anticipates this problem. Almost with the same breath with which he tells us that the Spirit will be in us, alive and at work, and that he will be in us, alive and at work, he tells us that something else is expected of us, namely, that we shall keep his commandments. This is how we demonstrate our connection with him, our love for him.

His commandments are not the commandments of Sinai. In John there is really only one: *"Love one another as I have loved you."* This commandment is in an obvious sense impossible to fulfill, but it gives us a standard by which to examine and judge what we believe to be the promptings of the God within us. We also have the story of Jesus' life and death, and we can ask how what we see or hear within ourselves fits with the meaning and call of that story.

We can turn, that is, from our own internal experience—where we cannot always keep straight the line between our self-centered desires and

"You in Me, and I in You"   167

the urgings of God—to Jesus' life and words, to his story and his teaching, as a ground upon which to understand the voices we hear within us. He is telling us always to come back to this haunting and powerful question: Do we love one another as he loves us?

Jesus is establishing here a vision of the life his followers are to lead: we shall know that God is within us, as a saving and guiding force; we shall recognize that we may mistake our own fallen impulses for the leadings of that God; we shall be able to turn in self-criticism to the story of Jesus itself, and to the community he established, the Church—including this very Church of the Mediator—for correction and enlightenment.

For this church, our church, is the place where we can hear the music of the soul that calls us into life, as the music of this passage does.

Thanks be to God.

Amen

In conversations over the years I have learned that for many people it is much easier to connect with one of the three Persons of God than with the others: some connect easily with the Father, but not the Son or the Spirit, others with the Son but not the other two, still others find the Spirit the most accessible. I have not taken a poll, but my sense is that to many people the Spirit seems less important or less available or less comprehensible than the other two. This makes sense in a way: of the Father we know that he is the Creator of all, and of the Son we have the long and compelling narrative of the Gospel. In a general way, we know about creation because we do a little creating ourselves, and we know about fathers and sons from our own experience.

But the Spirit? We have no image or narrative of the Spirit to give shape to our experience and imagination.

What is the Spirit, then? As Jesus tells us in the Nicodemus story, we know that the Spirit is breathing, moving, alive. Is the Spirit, then, the immediate and active presence of God within us, in an eternal now: without a history, without a story, without commandments, without any conceptual apparatus at all—living, moving, prompting, invisible but felt, like the wind?

24

The Mustard Seed

The passage that follows consists of a series of parables or images describing the kingdom of heaven. The kingdom is like a mustard seed, like yeast, like a treasure buried in a field, like a merchant in search of a fine pearl, like a fishing net in which many kinds of fish are caught, good and bad.

Why does Jesus use so many images? Why does he use these images in particular? And why does he use them in this order?

Where are we in this story?

The Gospel of Matthew 13:31–33, 44–49a

He put before them another parable: "The kingdom of heaven is like a mustard seed that someone took and sowed in his field; it is the smallest of all the seeds, but when it has grown it is the greatest of shrubs and becomes a tree, so that the birds of the air come and make nests in its branches."

He told them another parable: "The kingdom of heaven is like yeast that a woman took and mixed in with three measures of flour until all of it was leavened.

"The kingdom of heaven is like treasure hidden in a field, which someone found and hid; then in his joy he goes and sells all that he has and buys that field.

"Again, the kingdom of heaven is like a merchant in search of fine pearls; on finding one pearl of great value, he went and sold all that he had and bought it.

"Again, the kingdom of heaven is like a net that was thrown into the sea and caught fish of every kind; when it was full, they drew it ashore, sat down, and put the good into baskets but threw out the bad. So it will be at the end of the age. The angels will come out and separate the evil from the righteous."

The Church of the Mediator, July 27, 2008

May the words of my mouth and the meditations of my heart be always acceptable in thy sight, O Lord, my strength and my redeemer.

TODAY'S GOSPEL CONSISTS OF a set of five little parables, beginning with the mustard seed and ending with the fishing net, each one telling us what the kingdom of heaven is like.

Notice that Jesus does not tell us directly what the kingdom actually *is*, but tells us instead what it is *like*, in a series of images or comparisons. The reason is of course that what he means by the kingdom is strange, new, divine, and life changing—a manifestation of the holy force that animates the universe—and it cannot just be described in ordinary language. Jesus knows he cannot say what the kingdom *is* in human terms, so he says what it is *like*, using these images.

The Mustard Seed

First he compares the kingdom of heaven to a mustard seed. This seed starts out almost infinitesimally small but becomes a luxuriant plant, big enough to offer a nesting place to birds.

This image of natural growth is as normal and familiar as anything could be—we are of course surrounded by plants and we know how they grow—but it is also amazing, in a sense unbelievable. Our world does not have to have plants, or any other form of organic life. It could be like the moon, a dead rock. The beauty and power of the Creation as we know it, full of life and fruitfulness, is a gift, a constant miracle.

It makes sense to say that the kingdom of heaven is like a mustard seed. God's life in us often begins very small indeed, perhaps when a young couple decides that now that they have a baby they should go to a church. Maybe it turns out that they don't like what they see and go away; but maybe there is something in the air, something in the room, that draws them back. Probably not theology, not doctrine, not ideas, but the way people listen, perhaps, or the way they carry themselves when they receive communion or greet one another before or after church—a little piece of the kingdom of heaven. Then they say, we will come back next week. Then week leads into week, month into month, year into year, and they find themselves old, with grown children, and grandchildren too maybe, aware that the center of their whole life is what they found in the Church, in the sacraments, in the scriptures—in the kingdom of heaven. This is one way the kingdom can grow like a mustard seed: and like the mustard seed it is utterly familiar, utterly natural, and utterly amazing.

The Yeast

Jesus could stop with this image, but he does not. He goes on to tell us about the yeast that a woman works into a batch of flour, where it leavens the mass, filling it with bubbles of life.

Like the mustard seed, yeast starts very small and grows in a completely natural way to enliven the world. But there are new elements in this image, beyond those present in the image of the mustard seed. For one thing there is a human actor here, the woman who is using the yeast to make bread. And the yeast does not just grow; it acts on something else to transform it entirely, changing the flour and water from a kind of sticky paste into life-giving bread.

So the kingdom does not just happen out in the world somewhere, but works within us, like yeast, often at the hands of another, indeed often at the hands of a woman. It transforms who we are, our lives and souls, from the inside out.

The Treasure

But Jesus does not stop here either. Now he says that the kingdom is like the man who finds a treasure, buries it deep to keep it safe, then sells all he has so he can acquire the land where it is hidden.

This image makes its own additions. It implies a world with a complex economy, with a scale of value measured in money ("treasure"), and with rules of property too. It also imagines a human actor who is capable of highly self-interested planning and strategy.

This sequence of three images in a sense recapitulates the process of Creation itself: first we get nature (the seed), then nature acted on by a human being (the yeast), then a whole economy and society (the treasure).

In this last scene the human being is a person who wants to become rich. It would be easy to see this impulse as wholly inappropriate in an image of the kingdom. Is it really all about money and greed?

There is of course something in that objection, maybe a lot, but I think it misses what is really important in this parable, which is that this story carries us inside the head and heart of a person who is affected by the kingdom, here the man with the treasure. In this parable, that is, Jesus is telling us what it is like to be touched by the kingdom. It is like seeing an unbelievable treasure, and knowing that it is worth more than everything else you have, than anything thing you want, or might ever want. It is precious beyond words and beyond imagining.

The Pearl

The image of the pearl works much the same way, but this time the human actor is a merchant, an expert in pearls, a connoisseur of pearls, a person for whom pearls are everything. He knows pearls, and how to judge them; and to him the kingdom of heaven is like a pearl beyond all the pearls on earth.

We seem, then, to be getting some idea of the way this sequence works. Each image adds elements missing in the ones before, and as they proceed they produce a fuller and fuller picture of the natural and human world in which the kingdom will have its life, and of course a fuller sense of the kingdom too.

The Fishing Net

But now Jesus surprises us, and in a highly disconcerting way: for he introduces us to another aspect of the world—though maybe not exactly part of the Creation—namely, the reality of human sinfulness and its consequences. For at the crucial moment in the story the fishermen divide up the fish, keeping the good ones and throwing away the bad ones. In case we do not get the point, Jesus tells us that this is like what will happen at the end times, when angels will come to separate out the evil people from the good, and throw them into the furnace.

This is a real shock, full of threat. What are we to do with this sudden irruption of eternal damnation into the sequence of relatively comfortable images to which we have been exposed?

For us the whole idea of damnation is a difficult one to accept. Will people really be punished for ever and ever because of things they did that were bad? Is that something God the Father will really do, the Father who loved us so much that he sent us his Son to live among us and die for us? Is it what Jesus would do, Jesus who was so full of love for us, for all of us?

Obviously this is a deep theological question we cannot hope to resolve in a few minutes, or maybe ever.

But perhaps it is worth saying, as these parables themselves show, that there has to be judgment in life. Judgment about the amount of yeast, and how long to let it work; judgment about the value of the treasure or of the pearl, and the value of everything else one has; judgment too about our own growth as Christians. For our growth cannot be as unselfconscious and automatic as that of the mustard seed; it must be shaped to meet God's love and desire. We must judge and be judged too.

I am sure we are judged by God. It matters to him whether we love God and our neighbor with our whole heart. He is pained when we do not.

But real and deep as our failings and defects and sins are, I do not think that God will reject any of us for these things, and throw us away, if we confess from our hearts and turn to him. For we know that he loves us, all of us. As Paul said, "Christ Jesus came into the world to save sinners." And in today's reading from Romans Paul says that nothing, nothing at all, can separate us from the love of Christ (Romans 8:35).

On the other hand, it is in our power to reject God and his love for us. In this we are different from the mustard seed or the bird or the pearl. We have that power. This is an aspect of human freedom. What is more, we know that we do separate ourselves from God, over and over. As we say in the Confession, we do not love him with our whole heart; we do not love our neighbors as ourselves.

So how are we to understand the image of the fish being thrown away? Maybe the point is something like this. When we are told about the bad fish being thrown out, and told too what Jesus says about the judgment at the end of time, perhaps the idea is that we should come to see more clearly, and feel more deeply, our own sinfulness, our own exposure to judgment, our own danger; but that we should at the same time become more fully aware of the great need, the infinite need, that we therefore have, that the whole fallen Creation has, for the redeeming presence of Jesus himself: the presence that is in fact with us. The message is that we cannot get to the kingdom by ourselves—and we don't have to.

Jesus is the embodiment of the love of God. We know that it is he, the very person who is reminding us of our defects and danger, to whom we can turn, out of our awareness of our fallen nature and in confidence that he will accept all those who truly turn to him.

In the end it is his life and death and Resurrection, his presence now among us in this very church, that shows us more than anything else what the kingdom of heaven is like.

Amen

In this passage Matthew collects five parables and arranges them in a way that gives them a dramatic meaning.

Is this pattern Matthew's contribution, or are we to think that Jesus himself arranged them this way? Each of the parables can be found in the other two synoptic Gospels, those of Mark and Luke, but not in this arrangement. If so, the arrangement is the work of Matthew—substantially aided by those who compiled the lectionary (which omitted the section that contains Jesus' interpretation of the parable of the sower, which began the whole series of parables). Does this fact affect our sense of the sacredness of the text and its meaning? Properly so?

There is a related, more basic issue: it is commonly thought that all three of the synoptic Evangelists used a common source consisting of a set of Jesus' sayings that had been handed down to them, without much if any narrative context. The Evangelists add the story and arrange the materials. What does this compositional history, if it is correct, do to our sense of the sacredness of the Gospels more generally? To our sense of its origin in Jesus himself?

One way to think of it is to conceive of the Evangelists themselves as inspired by the Holy Spirit, so that even if they did not have direct access to Jesus' actual words, or to the context in which he uttered them, the text is still sacred, in some people's view still "inerrant." But that is what a lawyer would call a conclusory argument, one in which one's conclusions are buried in one's premises. It is hard to see how one could prove or disprove it.

Another way to respond is to recognize that we do not have access to all the information that the Evangelists had before them. The idea of their complete dependence on a collection of Jesus' sayings is itself a kind of conclusory supposition, a way of thinking that makes things simpler than they are. Maybe they had lots of information that we do not, including firsthand eyewitness testimony. After all, if Jesus died in the year 30, and Mark's Gospel was written thirty years later, there would have been a great many people still alive who had known Jesus personally. The Gospel would be in this respect like a book written in 2010 about events that occurred in 1980, which of course lots of people still remember. Even the Gospel of John, written near the end of the first century, would be no farther from the events described than a book written in 2010 about Pearl Harbor. So maybe the Gospels do rest upon eyewitness testimony far more than has been supposed. (A book that persuasively develops this line of thought is Richard Bauckham's *Jesus and the Eyewitnesses*.)

There is still another way to think of it, which is to recognize that the Evangelists were not historians in the modern sense, nor were they trying to be, but writers trying to capture the meaning of Jesus as fully as they could: the meaning of his life, of his death, of his Resurrection, of what he said and how he said it. As someone once said, they were not biographers but theologians.

Something I think the Evangelists all to a large degree do succeed in capturing, though each in a somewhat different way, is suggested by the phrase, "how he said it." For Jesus' way of confounding, puzzling, distressing, challenging, confusing, as well as sometimes comforting, his interlocutors is just as important as the explicit conceptual substance of what he says. Think of Nicodemus, for example, or the rich young man. One could imagine an interesting book—of theology not biography—with the title *What Was It Like to Talk with Jesus?*

We might each ask ourselves that very question, not only from the point of view of the original disciples, with whom Jesus talked in the flesh, but from our own point of view as well, for he still speaks to us, in the Gospels themselves and in other ways as well. What *is* it like to talk with Jesus?

25

"Who Do You Say I Am?"

Here we have still another story about Peter, this time telling us about the moment when he declares that Jesus is the Messiah, "the Son of the Living God." How do you suppose that Peter knows this, and the other disciples do not? Why in fact does Jesus ask him, and the other disciples, who they think he is? What does this say about Jesus himself and his relationship with his friends?

Where are we in this story?

> *The Gospel of Matthew 16:13–20*
>
> Now when Jesus came into the district of Caesarea Philippi, he asked his disciples, "Who do people say that the Son of Man is?" And they said, "Some say John the Baptist, but others Elijah, and still others Jeremiah or one of the prophets."
>
> He said to them, "But who do you say that I am?" Simon Peter answered, "You are the Messiah, the Son of the living God."
>
> And Jesus answered him, "Blessed are you, Simon son of Jonah! For flesh and blood has not revealed this to you, but my Father in heaven. And I tell you, you are Peter, and on this rock I will build my church, and the gates of Hades will not prevail against it. I will give you the keys of the kingdom of heaven, and whatever you bind on earth will be bound in heaven, and whatever you loose on earth will be loosed in heaven."
>
> Then he sternly ordered the disciples not to tell anyone that he was the Messiah.

The Church of the Mediator, August 24, 2008

May the words of my mouth and the meditations of my heart be always acceptable in thy sight, O Lord, my strength and my redeemer.

The more I have thought about today's Gospel the stranger it seems. Let's start with the two questions Jesus asks: "Who do the people say I am?" and "Who do you say I am?"

These may seem like familiar questions, but it is not clear to me exactly why Jesus is asking them. One possibility is that he is like a modern politician trying to check out his image: "What are they saying about me? What do *you* think?" But I don't think Jesus is doing that. He is not interested in damage control, nor does he want to shape who he is to meet the wishes of the public.

Another possibility, which I offer a bit tentatively, is that Jesus asks these questions because he is not wholly sure of his own identity and his role in the world. He knows that he is different from other people; he knows that he has a special relation to God, whom he refers to as his Father; he knows that he has extraordinary powers, including the power to expel demons and cure the sick. He knows too that Satan has tempted him, in ways that assume that he has powers that only God would have.

But I am not sure he knows fully who he is or exactly how his character and destiny will ultimately be realized, in his Crucifixion, Resurrection, and Ascension. How could he know these things? He is after all among other things a fully human person—once a baby and then a boy—living out a life in real time, with real people, and with expectations formed by his prior experience.

The very fact that there has never been anyone like him, that he is something completely new, means that he is faced with an infinitely special version of the familiar human problem, one that we all have, of self-discovery and self-understanding.

We saw Jesus engage in self-discovery last week, in his conversation with the Canaanite woman who asked him to heal her suffering daughter (Matthew 15:21–28). He responded to her first in a way that reflected the ugly cultural biases with which he was raised. He rejected her appeal and even called her a dog! But when she stubbornly insisted on her own reality and value, he came to see her as a full human being, and treated her that way too, instantly curing her daughter. In this passage Jesus himself is shown engaged in a process of change. We can watch him learn.

So Jesus' questions here make sense. He is asking who the people think he is because he is not totally sure himself.

He is told that some people think he is John the Baptist, others think he is Elijah, others Jeremiah or another of the prophets. The "people" are naturally comparing Jesus with what they know from their own cultural tradition, and seeing him in those terms.

But Jesus is not one of those prophets. We know that. On the other hand he is like them, for he is presenting to the world the truth of God's word. In a sense he is like them a thousand times over. So what the people say is imperfect, but it points in the right direction. It confirms Jesus' sense of his extraordinary nature and mission, without actually defining it. He is Elijah to the millionth power.

Jesus then puts his question to his disciples, asking them, *"Who do you say I am?"* Again I think he is genuinely interested in the answer. These are the people who know him best, after all. Maybe they will say something that will point in the right direction too.

What Peter tells him is, "You are the Messiah, the Son of the Living God." Jesus instantly responds with a powerful affirmation: *"Blessed are you, Simon son of Jonah. For flesh and blood has not revealed this to you, but my Father in heaven."*

I think that when Peter says that Jesus is the Messiah, Jesus is at first taken aback—Can it be?? But almost instantly he sees that this claim is in a deep way true, though he has never quite said it or known it. Jesus is here confirming the power of Peter's insight, his grasp of essential truth, which enables him to see and say what no one else can say.

But there is a complication, for many of the overtones and connotations of the term *messiah* do not actually apply to Jesus. Peter, like "the people," gets it partly right and partly wrong.

In the Hebrew Bible the word *messiah* (which in Hebrew means simply "anointed one") is mainly used to refer to the anointed kings of Israel. Peter's other phrase, "the son of God," is also a traditional term for describing a king in the line of David. So the implication of what Peter says is that Jesus will be a king, in particular a king like David, the great warrior who united the two kingdoms of Israel. The biblical connotations of the term are reinforced by the view, popular in Jesus' own day, that the Messiah would be a military leader, who would rescue Israel from its oppression at the hands of the Romans. He is to be a man of power in the world.

But this was not at all true of Jesus, who instead of leading a conquering army was ignominiously tortured to death as a criminal. In fact, in the rest of the Gospel story Jesus will transform what is meant by *messiah* into something radically different from anything Peter could possibly have meant: for Jesus the Messiah is the prince of peace, the one who dies on the cross for the sins of the whole world. He is the active principle of love for all people, especially the poor and the powerless.

This transformation in fact begins immediately after the scene we have been discussing, for it just at this point that Matthew tells us that Jesus began to reveal to his disciples that he would have to go to Jerusalem, where he would suffer, be killed, and rise from the dead. Jesus could suddenly see the new kind of Messiah he was going to be.

So both "the people" and Peter get it partly right, but partly wrong, and it is where they are wrong that Jesus will be most fully unique and distinctive.

So how about us? What is this story telling or showing us, about our own lives?

Think again of Jesus' two questions. Would we ever ask our friends, as Jesus did, *"Who do people say I am? Who do you say I am?"* If we did, why would we? What kind of answer would we expect? As you think about actually asking such questions, you may increasingly feel that they are scary—and why would that be?

If you did ask someone, *"Who do you say I am?"* they might say your name, as if that defined you; or maybe describe your job, as if that defined you; or maybe list your skills or social attributes, as if they defined you.

But who could say who you really are? Really, in your soul, at your center? Some people might see it, or part of it, but they could not really say it. No one can.

This is partly a question of the limits of language, of what can ever be said. But it is not just that. We do a lot to keep our inner selves private, hidden, secret. We share them selectively, for we may be misunderstood or hurt.

But never to share our inner selves, our deepest identity, would be a failure of life.

So in our own lives it is a question, just as it was for Jesus: How do we discover our identities, our inner selves? How, and to whom, do we reveal them? How do we attain and make manifest our own destinies?

For Jesus the center of the self that he was discovering and expressing was his identity as God, which is of course not true of us. But I think we are each in our own way at least a little like Jesus: for every single person in this room has a secret inner self; a touch of the divine; a call; a gift; a quality of soul—something at the center of us. Though we are not "all God," like Jesus, we do have a piece of God within us. But I imagine that most of us don't quite know what it is, or how to describe or reveal it. Maybe we are afraid to look.

We want both to protect this center, this spring of life and meaning—for this is where we can be most injured—and to discover it and share it, so far as we can, with others. This sharing of course does not have to be in grand ways: perhaps it can be in acts or words of kindness, in heartfelt prayers for others, in the honesty that recognizes our deepest commitments, in the courage to stand up for another, or simply in a touch or look of love or compassion.

As Jesus had to learn that he had God within him, then, and how to live out of that Presence and what it meant, we do too. As the Quakers say, there is "that of God in every person." Our task is to discover and reveal that Presence within us, to be true to it, and at the same time to respond to that Presence in others.

We cannot predict where our effort to discover and reveal the holy force within us will take us, perhaps any more than Jesus could. Maybe to a crucifixion of our own.

But if we can learn to live out of that deepest part of our soul, where it is connected to the Source of all Being, the principle of love at the heart of the universe, we shall have a life of a wholly new kind. This new life is the promise Jesus makes us.

How might we begin to live this way? Perhaps by having the courage to ask our friends, our closest friends: *Who do the people say I am? Who do you say I am*?

Amen

The idea that Jesus is engaged in a process of change and growth may be hard to accept, but I think it is true. In a sense he had to be, if he was ever an infant, a toddler, a little boy, an adolescent, a young man working as a carpenter: in each stage of life he had things to learn, mistakes to make, powers to discover. He had to learn and grow, if he was fully human, and he had to be fully human if his life and death were to mean what they did. His suffering on the cross was real suffering, human suffering, like our own; his fear of crucifixion was likewise like our own fear. This shared suffering is central to the promise of the Resurrection that follows.

This line of thought can lead us into idle speculation, however, which is I think to be resisted: it can lead us to ask whether Jesus ever experienced frustration or envy as a child, for example, or was greedy, or cheated at games, or wished that his family had more food or a better house, or felt a kind of rivalry with his brothers. These things are unknowable and in any event do not matter. To pursue them is to trivialize Jesus himself.

But to say that he was capable of discovery and growth, as I think the Gospel reveals, does not belittle him at all, but rather recognizes a deep truth of his nature, a truth that can in fact add to our sense of gratitude and amazement at his presence in the world and in our lives.

What happens if we look at our own lives and ask: Are we learning? Are we changing? How, and how do we know?

26

"Seventy Times Seven"

This Gospel passage presents one of the most difficult issues for any Christian, the duty of forgiveness. In the prayer that Jesus taught us, we ask to be forgiven "as we forgive others." This has always been deeply troubling to me, for I know how weakly and thinly I forgive, how often I refuse to forgive. But the duty of forgiveness is primary in Jesus' mind. We are not to pray to be forgiven *"despite our failures to forgive others"*–which is surely what most of us would like to do–but *"as we forgive others,"* a prayer that must make us deeply uncomfortable. Apparently, to be forgiven we must forgive.

How can this be? We all know how incomplete and pale our own acts of forgiveness are. Are they really to be the measure of the forgiveness we receive?

As Peter asks in the passage below, how much are we to forgive? Seven times? Or, as Jesus tells him in the NRSV, *"Not seven times, but, I tell you, seventy-seven times"*? Or, as he says, more severely, in the King James Version quoted in the chapter title, *"I say not unto thee, until seven times: but until seventy times seven"*?[1]

---

1. Which translation is right? I think they are both plausible, and in any event they are saying much the same thing: forgive more times than you can possibly imagine doing it.

"Seventy Times Seven"

The Gospel of Matthew 18:21–35

Then Peter came and said to him, "Lord, if another member of the church sins against me, how often should I forgive? As many as seven times?"

Jesus said to him, "Not seven times, but, I tell you, seventy-seven times. For this reason the kingdom of heaven may be compared to a king who wished to settle accounts with his slaves. When he began the reckoning, one who owed him ten thousand talents was brought to him; and, as he could not pay, his lord ordered him to be sold, together with his wife and children and all his possessions, and payment to be made.

"So the slave fell on his knees before him, saying, 'Have patience with me, and I will pay you everything.' And out of pity for him, the lord of that slave released him and forgave him the debt. But that same slave, as he went out, came upon one of his fellow slaves who owed him a hundred denarii; and seizing him by the throat, he said, 'Pay what you owe.' Then his fellow slave fell down and pleaded with him, 'Have patience with me, and I will pay you.' But he refused; then he went and threw him into prison until he would pay the debt.

"When his fellow slaves saw what had happened, they were greatly distressed, and they went and reported to their lord all that had taken place. Then his lord summoned him and said to him, 'You wicked slave! I forgave you all that debt because you pleaded with me. Should you not have had mercy on your fellow slave, as I had mercy on you?' And in anger his lord handed him over to be tortured until he would pay his entire debt.

"So my heavenly Father will also do to every one of you, if you do not forgive your brother or sister from your heart."

THE CHURCH OF THE MEDIATOR, SEPTEMBER 14, 2008

May the words of my mouth and the meditations of my heart be always acceptable in thy sight, O Lord, my strength and my redeemer.

I HAVE TO BEGIN by saying that I think Jesus' teaching about forgiveness—"seventy times seven!" in the King James Version—is about the hardest thing he has to say, at least for me. In difficulty it ranks with loving your enemies, praying for those who despitefully use you, and loving God with all your heart and mind and soul.

When he tells us to forgive those who injure us, Jesus is calling not for simple adherence to a moral rule of some kind, like telling the truth or not stealing, but for a complete transformation of what it means to be a person. And what he asks seems plainly beyond our human powers.

There is of course more than one kind of forgiveness. Today I want to talk about two: the first is very hard; the second is just about impossible.

Here is the first kind. Suppose a person at work opens your desk and takes twenty dollars that he or she finds there. You know it is missing and have no idea who has taken it. But one afternoon, just about quitting time, the culprit comes to you, shamefaced, and confesses that he took your money. He pays it back, says he is sorry from his heart, and asks for your forgiveness.

How do you respond? You might be irritated and surprised and offended, but I think most of us would be able to forgive him, or at least to try to do so. The wrongdoer is seeking to reestablish a relationship he has broken, or rendered false, and to put it on an honest basis. You are confident that he is sincere because he could have got away with the theft, but chose to turn himself in.

If we think about it, we can see why it is so important that we do forgive such a person. What he is doing is very hard, psychologically and morally: he is revealing something shameful about himself, and exposing himself to rejection and contempt. You can really hurt him: practically, if you turn him in to the boss; emotionally, if you reject his offer of himself. He has put himself in your hands.

This is in fact a sacred moment, a moment in which a trusting soul is trying to do the right thing in circumstances of peril. It really matters whether we respond with acceptance and love, or with rejection.

So of course we must do our best to forgive him, and welcome him to the world of trust and hope. This may be very hard, for we have been injured—our own sense of trust in our fellow workers, in other people generally, has been damaged, maybe severely—but we should try. We might even invite him to come to church with us.

His asking forgiveness, and our granting it, open up new possibilities for the presence and life of the Spirit, for both of us. Forgiveness may thus do more than restore a relationship; it may transform it, deepening our sense of trust and shared humanity.

But this is a relatively easy kind of forgiveness: the injury is not very great and the wrongdoer both accepts responsibility for what he has done and actively seeks our forgiveness. He wants the relation restored, and so do we. Our forgiveness may well be imperfect, but we can at least imagine it, wish for it.

There is a much harder kind of forgiveness. Suppose for example that the injury the person confesses to having inflicted is a terrible one, simply terrible. Imagine that our brother or uncle confesses that he sexually abused one of our children, for example—something that I hope has never happened to anyone in this room. This crime can blight the child's entire life, from the center out: damaging their capacity to form relations of trust and hope and intimacy with other people; injuring the sense of self-worth upon which a full life depends; and preventing them from achieving the kind of self-realization that is everyone's right. While therapy can help a child who has suffered such abuse, it cannot make it simply go away. The injury is permanent and terrible.

So this man has damaged the life of our beloved child at the center. He admits it and asks for forgiveness. Do we forgive him? Can we possibly want to restore *that* relationship? Is this what Jesus really wants us to do?

Or suppose the person is simply not repentant at all. He does not ask for forgiveness from us. He has no interest in us or what we feel, no interest in a restored relationship with us. Say he is caught stealing money from our desk and is completely unfazed. Or when we confront him with the lies he told about us, he simply laughs. Or, to put this case together with the one given just a moment ago, he is a child abuser who, like so many, justifies himself by saying that the child asked for it. It was really the child's fault. Or he just smirks at us, with no recognition that what he has done is horrible.

Can we imagine forgiving a person of this kind? Why and how? Here there is no sacred moment of trust and self-exposure, as when the person confesses and asks forgiveness. He does not put himself in our hands. In a real sense there is nothing to respond to, no possibility of a restored relationship, let alone a transformed one.

So does Jesus really want us to forgive in these cases where forgiveness seems impossible? I think he does, in part because he has in mind a different kind of forgiveness: not the restoration of a relationship, but simply "letting go" of a sense of wrong and injury.

I don't know about the Aramaic that Jesus actually spoke, but in the Greek in which the Gospel is written the word for *forgiveness* does not mean the restoration of a relation of trust, but something like "throw it away." In the case of a debt, like the one in the parable that Jesus tells, forgiveness means simply canceling the debt, tearing up the note and the mortgage.

I think Jesus is asking us to "let go" not just when it is easy, but when the wrong is so horrible that we cannot imagine forgiving it at all and the perpetrator is so wedded to his violation that he cannot see or does not care that it is wrong.

Think of what Jesus himself was able to say on the cross: *"Father, forgive them; for they know not what they do"* (Luke 23:34). The crucifiers were torturing Jesus to death, and they were not repenting. Yet Jesus forgives them. He wants us to do likewise.

That I think is clear. But we can still ask: Why does Jesus want us to do that? Who is really benefited by such a "letting go"? Is forgiveness for the wrongdoer's sake or for our own?

Maybe we are to do it for ourselves. Our act of forgiveness will mean nothing to the smirking bully, the torturer, the child-abusing uncle. The point is rather to clear our own soul of the constant sense of injury and the need for revenge. We are to forgive so that we do not spend our lives obsessing about the wrongs that have been done us—even the serious and undoubted wrongs.

The point of forgiveness, then, is to free us, so that we can live in the present moment, with other people. It is to make us able to join the dance of life with ease and grace. To obsess about wrongs, even serious ones, is a waste of life.

But maybe forgiveness can sometimes be for the other person as well, even if he does not recognize that he needs it. Here I think of the way that Martin Luther King would talk about nonviolent resistance: for him, standing up to brutality was a way of speaking to the perpetrators themselves, appealing to that piece of God that lived within each of them. Maybe when they see us not fighting back against the violence they are inflicting, but forgiving them, or when they remember it later, they will learn something important—about our humanity, about the injustice of what they are doing, maybe even about their own humanity.

But can we do this? Can we forgive where the wrong is terrible or where the wrongdoer is unrepentant? It is hard even to imagine. It looks as if Jesus is asking us to do something we cannot do. In an important sense I think that is true. So how are we to respond to this situation?

First a general point: the fact that we find it so hard to imagine ourselves forgiving in the way that Jesus forgives is itself a sign that the transformation he is bringing into the world is radical beyond our imagination. It is really a transformation of everything: of our way of conceiving of ourselves and others; of our way of framing hopes and expectations; of our way of thinking about what is ours, including our own bodies and our lives. Jesus is asking us to be centers of boundless, unimaginable love, love that is truly unconditional just as his is. We really are asked to love our enemies and to forgive what they do to us and to those we love.

How can we do this? I don't know about you, but I am sure that I cannot forgive as Jesus wants me to. When I am injured there is always some residue of resentment and anger. I can try hard, but I cannot just send it all away.

This is of course not the only impossible thing Jesus asks of us. I cannot love God with my whole heart and mind and being, either; I cannot love my neighbor as myself. It is puzzling and paradoxical, but nonetheless true, that impossibility of this kind is an essential quality of what Jesus demands of us.

But it is the teaching of our faith, and Jesus' gift to us, that we are not alone in facing these demands and our certain failure to meet them. We have Jesus to show us that this kind of forgiveness is possible, at least for him, and thus to give us something to strive for; we have a heavenly Father who will forgive us when we recognize and confess our sins, including our own failures to forgive; and we have the Church, including this church, this community of saints and sinners, to help us support and forgive each another as we each struggle with the impossible effort to attain perfect love and forgiveness.

Amen

In the sermon, I draw attention to the ways in which we are told that to be forgiven we must ourselves forgive. This is indeed part of it. But in this parable Jesus shows us something else. He explains in a different way why we should forgive, and, more than that, how it might be possible for us to forgive: it is because we are already forgiven.

In the Gospel story it is the fact that the servant has been forgiven by his lord that makes his refusal to forgive his fellow servant such a deep and even puzzling wrong. If he has been forgiven himself, he should certainly forgive others, especially when his own debt or offense is so much the greater of the two. This is obvious.

Jesus is telling us that this is our case. We have been offered forgiveness, if we only ask for it from our hearts. Like the servant in the story it is obvious that we ought to forgive and obvious too that we should find forgiveness within our capacity.

What do we do about the fact that we still do not want to forgive, still find forgiveness hard or impossible?

27

Healing the Leper

The passage below tells the story of one of Jesus' many healings, this time of a leper, who was unclean under the law of Leviticus. Jesus touches him, thus contaminating himself under Jewish law; but when the man is cured, he orders him to take part in the ritual of cleansing before a priest. Why does Jesus at one moment disregard the law, and at another compel compliance with it?

He also tells the man to say nothing about what has happened, a command that the man disobeys. Why does Jesus command his silence?

As we read this story of the healer and the sick man, where do we find ourselves within it?

The Gospel of Mark 1:40–45

A leper came to him begging him, and kneeling he said to him, "If you choose, you can make me clean." Moved with pity, Jesus stretched out his hand and touched him, and said to him, "I do choose. Be made clean!"

Immediately the leprosy left him, and he was made clean. After sternly warning him he sent him away at once, saying to him, "See that you say nothing to anyone; but go, show yourself to the priest, and offer for your cleansing what Moses commanded, as a testimony to them."

> But he went out and began to proclaim it freely, and to spread the word, so that Jesus could no longer go into a town openly, but stayed out in the country; and people came to him from every quarter.

St. Andrew's Church, February 15, 2009

May the words of my mouth and the meditations of my heart be always acceptable in thy sight, O Lord, my strength and my redeemer.

What exactly was the condition of the man whom Jesus healed in the story we just heard from Mark's Gospel? He is said to be a "leper," but we are told by scholars that he almost certainly did not suffer from the modern disease we call leprosy, which probably did not even exist at that time. He must have had one of another set of skin ailments—ranging from infections to eczema, maybe including acne and various fungal afflictions as well—that were then regarded by Jewish law as pollutions.

Under the laws of Leviticus, a person who suffered from one of these conditions—some of which were curable, others not—was pronounced ceremonially unclean by the priest; his presence in a house contaminated it; and anyone who touched him had to be purified. He was in effect ejected from the community.

When we think what life was like in those days, especially for rural people who had to care for the animals and work the fields, all with little opportunity to wash, there were probably lots of people who were afflicted with one form or another of a skin condition thought to be unclean, and were consequently ostracized. For most people it was probably a life sentence.

So it is with the man who approaches Jesus. He is a kind of outcast or pariah.

He comes to Jesus to be cured, kneeling before him and saying, "If you choose, you can make me clean."

This is a wonderful gesture, expressing deep and unquestioning faith in Jesus' power. But it is also apparent that the man is at the same time not certain what Jesus will in fact choose to do. I hear in him the voice of one who has been so often rejected by the world that he does not really expect anyone to help him at all. No one ever has.

It is to this complex utterance, full of faith but expecting nothing, that Jesus responds in a way that is utterly simple and utterly meaningful: he reaches out his hand to touch him and says, *"I do choose. Be made clean!"* And it was so.

It is striking that Jesus physically touches the man. Presumably he could have cured him just with words, or with a look. So why did he touch him? What does it mean, to the man, to Jesus, and to us?

It may help here to think of the power of touching in our own lives, especially its healing power. When we go to the doctor for an exam, it is important that he or she actually touch us: listen to our lungs and hearts, feel our belly, look in our ears and eyes. These touchings, done with concern and care, are an important part of medical practice and healing, perhaps more than we often recognize.

But touch is important not only to healing. Think of a young mother holding a baby, or a child—as Mary once held Jesus—and touching him in love. Nothing in life is more important than such a touch. She is teaching her baby about love.

Just imagine a life without touching, in which no one had ever touched you. It would be a kind of hell. When no one touches the babies in overcrowded orphanages, they wither and die. The man in the story has been leading just this kind of life, a life without touch, without acceptance and caring. He has been without what Jesus gives him, the simple act of human touch, which both heals him and teaches him about love.

In touching the afflicted man, Jesus is telling us that while some people of course suffer from disease, including disfiguring disease, no one is contaminated, no one is polluted, no one is by nature unclean, and—whatever the law may say—we are never to treat them as if they were.

That I think is the main message of this Gospel reading. But there is even more to it, which may become apparent if we ask ourselves (always a good idea in reading the Gospel) exactly where we are within it.

One answer here is not very comforting, to say the least: that we are among those who reject and ostracize this man for his disease. For it is true that a lot of us tend to draw a sharp line between what we think of as the clean and the unclean, the diseased and the healthy, the accepted and the ostracized, sometimes without quite knowing it.

I think of my own response to people on the street who, like the man Jesus heals, are without homes, without food, without money, without the essentials of life and health. I may give a person a dollar or two, I may support the breakfast program, I may even spend a night at the shelter. But I do not, in the sense that Jesus does, touch them in love. I do not make their condition of ostracism my own as a stage in seeking to abolish it.

As for people suffering from disease, especially serious disease, we often turn away from them, even when they are members of our own families. We forget to call our friend who has Parkinson's; we put off visiting our parent suffering from early stage Alzheimer's; we leave the room of a dying person with a sense of relief at our return to the normal world—as if we do not know that someday it will be our turn.

This refusal or incapacity to love and accept others as they are is itself a kind of sickness, not a physical but a moral sickness. This means something perhaps surprising: that we are present in the story in a second way, not only as those who ostracize the afflicted, but as the afflicted person himself, who is in need of healing. For when we shrink from the poor, the homeless, the sick, the dying, drawing a line between them and us, afraid of contamination, we ourselves are truly afflicted, afflicted in our hearts, and truly in need of Christ's healing touch. And like the man in the story, we should ask him for it.

There is another feature of this story, which may enable us to find still a third place to stand within it. What I refer to is the fact that here Jesus shows us that he is fully human, as well as fully God.

Think of the act of touching itself. As I suggested earlier, if he were only God, momentarily disguised as a human being, I think he would feel no need to touch the man. But Jesus is a human being, with a human body and with human feelings. He is moved, as the text says, by his deep compassion for the man; and his touching him confirms both the reality of his own physical being and the possibility of physical connection with the man—and with us.

Jesus also reveals that he experiences what we would call "inner conflict" in much the same way we do. So at the moment of healing he is full of compassion for the sick man, eager to demonstrate his opposition to the law that makes the man a pariah, and comfortable doing so in public. But as soon as he has cured him, Jesus speaks to him harshly—the word literally means "with a snort"; he commands him to tell no one about what has happened, keeping it a secret; and he orders him to comply with the requirements that the book of Leviticus imposes on a person whose skin disease has been cured.

Jesus himself thus experiences an inner conflict with respect to the authority of Leviticus, which he first repudiates, in touching the man, then recognizes, in ordering his ritual purification; in his attitude towards the afflicted person, towards whom he first feels compassion, then something like irritation or anger; and with respect to his own public role as preacher and healer, which he first affirms, then wants to hide.

In making plain Jesus' full humanity, the Gospel story suggests that we might be present in it not only as those who shrink from disease and poverty, not only as those who are morally diseased themselves and need the touch of Jesus, but as those who can do what Jesus himself does, namely, reach out to others with a loving touch. The fact that he is like *us* means that we can strive to be like *him*.

So the real question this Gospel presents is this: Can we learn to act as Jesus did, to touch our neighbor in healing love and compassion? To recognize the full humanity and dignity of every person, as the Baptismal Covenant requires? How possibly can we do these things?

I have no easy answer, but it may help if we remind ourselves that it was in part to enable us to do these things—imperfectly, of course, as is our nature, but do them—that Christ came to live among us, and lives among us still.

For he does live in Gospel passages like this one, in the spoken Word, touching us this very morning through our ears; and he lives in the life of our church, in our acceptance and care for each other, including when we are sick in mind or body, including at the moment when we touch each other as we give one another the Peace of God; and he lives in the Eucharist itself, where he touches us once more in a physical way, as his body and blood become incorporated within our own.

So: when in a few moments we touch each other as we give one another God's peace, let us be conscious, if we can, that it is the Christ in each of us who is greeting the Christ in the other. When we celebrate the

Eucharist, let us be conscious, if we can, that Christ himself is present in the bread and wine, touching us and feeding us.

And let us pray that with his help we can learn to live as he would have us do.

Amen

Jesus seems to have had a hard time keeping himself secret. He warns the leper not to tell anyone, but, as one can well imagine, the warning has no effect whatever. After all, what is this man to say, who shows up one day completely cured of a long-term polluting disease? That it just went away overnight? He needs a better explanation than that.

What is more, if he is like the others whom Jesus cures, he is full of gratitude and love, as well as amazement, and no one can keep feelings like that bottled up.

So why does Jesus tell him to keep it quiet in the first place, especially when it is obvious that he won't do it? This is a version of a large question in Mark's Gospel, the technical term for which is the *Messianic Secret*. What the term refers to is a series of events in which Jesus either tells his disciples not to talk about him or deliberately refuses to reveal his nature to the people at large. It refers also to the scene in which Jesus tells the parable of the sower but explains it only to the disciples, saying that the reason is so that the people will not understand and be saved (Mark 4:11–12). The Secret is related to another feature of Mark's Gospel as well, which is that the disciples regularly do not understand what Jesus is telling them, however explicitly he does so. You may remember, for example, that in his version of the "walking on the water" passage, Mark tells us that the disciples did not understand what had happened at the feeding of the five thousand (Mark 6:52).

In all of these contexts Mark captures quite clearly the sense that Jesus is incompletely understood by the world, sometimes because he is incompletely revealed, sometimes because people just don't get it. This seems to me an extraordinarily acute piece of realism in Mark's work. If Jesus came your own life, as a fiery preacher and generally somewhat difficult personality, what would you make of him? You might love him, and follow him even to death. But would you understand that he is God incarnate, even if he told you? How possibly?

28

The Grain of Wheat

In this passage from John, Jesus foresees his own death. Perhaps as a way of explaining to himself what is about to happen, Jesus thinks of the grain of wheat, which must die to bear fruit. He shrinks from what is coming, then reconciles himself to it with the recognition that this is why he has come into the world.

But why must Jesus die, especially in this awful and cruel way? The fact that a seed must change its form in becoming a plant does not really explain why Jesus must be crucified. And what of us: we are to die to the world, he says, or at least we are to hate life in this world. Why is that, if the world is good because God made it? What is all this hating and dying?

The Gospel of John 12:20-33

Now among those who went up to worship at the festival were some Greeks. They came to Philip, who was from Bethsaida in Galilee, and said to him, "Sir, we wish to see Jesus."

Philip went and told Andrew; then Andrew and Philip went and told Jesus. Jesus answered them, "The hour has come for the Son of Man to be glorified. Very truly, I tell you, unless a grain of wheat falls into the earth and dies, it remains just a single grain; but if it dies, it bears much fruit. Those who love their life lose it, and those who hate their life in this world will keep it for eternal life. Whoever serves me must follow me, and where I am, there will my servant be also. Whoever serves me, the Father will honor. Now my soul is troubled. And what should I say—'Father, save me from this hour'? No, it is for this reason that I have come to this hour. Father, glorify your name."

Then a voice came from heaven, "I have glorified it, and I will glorify it again." The crowd standing there heard it and said that it was thunder. Others said, "An angel has spoken to him." Jesus answered, "This voice has come for your sake, not for mine. Now is the judgment of this world; now the ruler of this world will be driven out. And I, when I am lifted up from the earth, will draw all people to myself." He said this to indicate the kind of death he was to die.

THE CHURCH OF THE MEDIATOR, MARCH 29, 2009

May the words of my mouth and the meditations of my heart be always acceptable in thy sight, O Lord, my strength and my redeemer.

IN TODAY'S GOSPEL JESUS uses the immensely powerful image of the grain of wheat to talk about the great mystery he is facing, one that we in our own way all face too: the mystery of dying into life. *"Unless a grain of wheat falls into the earth and dies, it remains but a single grain; but if it dies, it bears much fruit."*

What does this image mean, and how is Jesus using it?

I thought of bringing a packet of seeds with me, and handing them out so that each of us would have a seed before us, a seed we could actually take home. I did not quite have the courage to do that, but let us imagine that we do each have a seed—a biggish one, maybe like a nasturtium seed or perhaps a squash or pumpkin seed.

What is that seed like? It is hard, with a nearly impermeable husk or outer layer. You cannot scratch it with your fingernail; you cannot really cut it even with a knife, beyond making a notch or two. It has life deep within it, which it is protecting; not of course the full life of the plant, with flower and fruit, but life nonetheless. A truly dead seed is brittle and friable, so that you can crumble it in your fingers.

If it could speak what would it say?

Perhaps something like this: "I like the way I am. I am safe—every living thing wishes for safety, and that is what I have. I am alive. I am secure. I am doing very well, thank you."

If you took your seed home and tossed it in a kitchen drawer, where you left it till next year, it would then be exactly the same: safe, alone, unchanging.

What does the seed like? It likes darkness and dryness and cold. It likes staying always the same.

What is it afraid of? Light and moisture and warmth, which would make it start to grow, whether it wanted to or not. The husk would thin out and become flexible, and finally split apart. A plant would then grow out into the world, first as a tiny green shoot; but with more water and light and warmth it would burst into flower—into squash flowers, say, or nasturtium flowers—to beautify and enrich the world.

When a seed "dies" in the sense Jesus means, then, it does not actually die, but the opposite: it experiences an almost unimaginable transformation into new life. Think of the desert bursting into bloom after a rain.

But this new life is also vulnerable to injury in a way that the seed was not: to cold, to drought, to blight, to destruction.

In this passage Jesus uses the image of the seed dying into life as a way of talking about three somewhat different things.

To start with, he is talking about his own impending death. When Philip and Andrew report to him that Greek-speaking Jews—Jews from outside Israel—want to speak to him, he sees immediately that this means that his hour of trial has come. For if he is well enough known to attract the attention of such foreigners, the powers of the political and religious establishment that he has been challenging will find his presence intolerable and put an end to him, or at least try to do so.

When Jesus utters the words about the seed, then, he is partly talking about himself. He probably does not know fully what the "death of the seed" will mean for him, but he can feel the life of what is to come starting within him. He is aware of his sudden vulnerability to pain and death. As he says, *"My soul is troubled."*

Of course he is troubled: he is about to undergo a transformation that he fears and cannot completely understand. It is only by an act of dramatic imagination that he can reconcile himself to it: *"Unless a grain of wheat falls into the earth and dies, it remains but a single grain; but if it dies, it bears much fruit."*

We can see what Jesus perhaps could not, that his Crucifixion is part of the most astonishing miracle in the history of the world. By his death into new life, Jesus flowers into his universal Church, which has been growing into transformed life around the world for two thousand years; he flowers into his church here, the Church of the Mediator; he flowers into his church in the heart of each one of us. By his dying into life, the whole world is alive in a new way.

Jesus also uses the image of the seed as a way of talking about us, about what we should do in our own lives. He tells us that we too should die into life, at the center of our being.

We too should convert what is dry, dark, and afraid within us into a life that is warm and growing, in a world of light and moisture. But just as was true for Jesus, this new life of ours will be open in a new way to injury at the hand of evil or of chance.

When we ask what this transformation can possibly mean for us, it might be helpful to see that we already have experience of transformations of this kind, in ourselves and others.

Think of a young couple who decide to get married. They love each other in ways they could never have imagined loving. They join together for the adventure of life. But in some sense they cannot possibly know what they are doing: what it will mean to live in intimacy and responsibility with another soul, for life. The old self will die away, the self of young love, and a new self will come to take its place, the self of enduring love. In the process each will be exposed in a wholly new way to joy, but also to the threat of grief and loss.

After a couple of years our couple discovers that they are to have a child. They can see and feel the new life, the life that will be their child, beginning to grow. But they cannot know—it is literally unimaginable—what it will mean to give birth to a new human life, a human soul, for which they are responsible. It will change their own lives completely, from the inside out. They will inhabit a different plane of existence. They will also become vulnerable in a wholly new way. They will learn to live outside their own bodies, wherever their child is. In a sense they will now never stop worrying.

We sometimes feel stirrings of new life deep within us, at the deepest part of our own souls. We feel the green shoot growing, the shell beginning to crack; perhaps we struggle against it, trying to cram ourselves back into an encapsulated life—less vulnerable, more safe. We become fearful. But then maybe, somehow, we give ourselves to the life within us—not perfectly or completely of course, for we are all deeply limited—but give ourselves, as well as we can.

To make these transformations we do not need to die on the cross, as Jesus did. But we do need to recognize that to move from the life of the seed to the life of fruit and flower is to go from a life that tries to avoid pain and suffering to a life that is necessarily open and vulnerable to these things. Life and love expose us to injury.

This is perhaps Jesus' hardest teaching, for himself as well as us: that the pain and suffering we naturally seek to avoid are necessary parts of the full life to which he calls us.

There are many kinds of suffering, and nothing we do can makes us safe from them. Even the seed can be burnt or desiccated. Indeed, if the seed does not burst into life—die into life, as we are called to do—it will dry up and wither away, or simply rot. In neither case will it ever have truly lived.

Jesus is calling us to be vulnerable to the special kind of pain to which we are exposed by love and hope: the pain of a full life.

Perhaps now we can see why Jesus talks in his strange way about hating life. We are of course not to hate the life we have been talking about, true life—the life of fruit and flower, light and warmth—but we *are* to hate, to struggle against, the side of us that denies or rejects what he offers. We are to hate the life that shrinks into the protection of a seedcase isolated in the dark, withering away.

The third thing Jesus uses the image of the seed to talk about is the mystery of our own physical death and the eternal life he promises us. What he means by eternal life must, I think, in the nature of things elude us. For the life of which he speaks, the life beyond this world, is as utterly unimaginable to us as the life of the flower and fruit would be to the seed lying in the dark drawer.

But we have seen the seeds of plants burst into life. We have also seen seeds burst into life in the marriage of our friends, in their parenthood, in the history of the Church, the history of this church. We can sometimes feel the green shoots moving and growing within us. We have seen Jesus die into even more abundant life. We live in hope of what we cannot know.

We are a little like the people who heard the voice of the Father speaking to Jesus from the sky. Was it thunder? Was it an angel? Was it the Father? What does it mean? We cannot fully know.

But we do know that we do not face the uncertainty, the vulnerability, of life alone. "Yea, though I walk through the valley of the shadow of death, I will fear no evil, for thou art with me."

Amen

One of the striking things in this story is way the voice from heaven is heard. We are told that this voice says, in response to Jesus' prayer to the Father that he glorify his name, "I have glorified it and will glorify it again." This a direct showing forth of the Father, on a parallel with what happened to Moses and Elijah in their meetings with God on Sinai. Yet it is heard by the people as something else: some think it is only thunder; others think it is angels speaking.

How often are we in the first group, do you suppose: present at a showing forth of God but thinking of what we observe as a purely natural phenomenon? We each have to pick our own places, but one possibility is the experience of seeing a child being born. Is this a purely natural process, driven and determined by DNA and "natural selection," or is it the manifestation of God himself on earth, creating a new human soul, full of infinite possibility and infinite value? Or how about the garden in our backyard, producing tomatoes and lettuce and corn: Is this just nature well managed, or is it a miracle? How about the peace we sometimes see on the face of a dying person? Or the smile from the heart with which a girl answering a cell phone expresses her realization that it is her beloved boyfriend calling?

Sometimes perhaps we see that it is angels speaking—maybe in all these cases. But do we ever see it as God, the principle of love and power at the center of the universe? If we did, could we survive the revelation?

29

The Resurrection of Jesus

There is no question harder, no question more important for the Christian, than how we are to understand and live with the Resurrection. As a physical fact it flies in the face of all experience. How can we believe it? As the story is told, it become apparent that the resurrected Jesus is not just a revived corpse, but transformed, heightened, and empowered. How can that possibly be?

What is more, the Resurrection is supposed to have changed everything, but there seems to be just as much evil in the world as there ever was.

What does the Resurrection mean?

The Gospel of Luke 24:36–49

While they were talking about this, Jesus himself stood among them and said to them, "Peace be with you." They were startled and terrified, and thought that they were seeing a ghost.

He said to them, "Why are you frightened, and why do doubts arise in your hearts? Look at my hands and my feet; see that it is I myself. Touch me and see; for a ghost does not have flesh and bones as you see that I have." And when he had said this, he showed them his hands and his feet.

While in their joy they were disbelieving and still wondering, he said to them, "Have you anything here to eat?" They gave him a piece of broiled fish, and he took it and ate in their presence.

Then he said to them, "These are my words that I spoke to you while I was still with you—that everything written about me in the law of Moses, the prophets, and the psalms must be fulfilled."

Then he opened their minds to understand the scriptures, and he said to them, "Thus it is written, that the Messiah is to suffer and to rise from the dead on the third day, and that repentance and forgiveness of sins is to be proclaimed in his name to all nations, beginning from Jerusalem. You are witnesses of these things. And see, I am sending upon you what my Father promised; so stay here in the city until you have been clothed with power from on high."

The Church of the Mediator, April 26, 2009

May the words of my mouth and the meditations of my heart be always acceptable in thy sight, O Lord, my strength and my redeemer.

IN THE PASSAGE WE just heard, Jesus suddenly appears to the disciples in Jerusalem, and tells them not to be afraid; he shows them the wounds in his hands and feet, to prove that it is really he who is there, not some apparition; he eats a piece of fish, to prove that he is really alive, in body; and then he teaches them the meaning of the scripture and of his life, telling them at the end to await the arrival of the Spirit in Jerusalem.

This is all completely familiar—we have heard the story again and again—but at the same time it is immensely mysterious.

Jesus' Resurrection is the center of our faith, the great event of Easter upon which all our hope is founded. But we understandably have a hard time answering the most basic questions about it. What was Jesus' Resurrection? What did it mean to his disciples? What does it mean to us?

We can start with what it was not. Jesus' Resurrection was not the mere resuscitation of a dead body, like the revival of Lazarus. Lazarus returned to life exactly as he had known it, in the same body; then, when his time came, he died, just as people always do. But in the Resurrection Jesus is completely transformed: in some sense he does have a physical body, as he shows by eating fish; but at the same time he is not subject to the usual laws of physics, as he demonstrates by appearing and disappearing mysteriously. When he is not with the disciples, no one knows where he is.

He who was dead is now alive; and his life has been amazingly transfigured.

Paul tells us, in his letter to the Corinthians, that if there were no Resurrection our whole faith would be empty (1 Corinthians 15:14).

I think this is true. If Jesus had done and said everything the Gospels say, including the miracles, but did not come back from death, he would be to us just another good man, maybe a uniquely good man, who was ultimately defeated by the forces of evil. We might want to imitate him, indeed we could have built a church upon what he left us, but we would at the same time ultimately expect to be defeated too.

Or consider this: if Jesus had lived to a ripe old age, died of the usual human causes, then come back to life for awhile and after that was taken bodily to heaven, even then would there not be something crucial missing from the story?

I think so, and that something is the Cross. For in fact Jesus did not just die, he was killed. He was killed by the only thing that could kill him, by all the evil in the world concentrated into one place and one moment in time. That evil includes our own evil, as we affirm when in the reading of the Passion we cry out, "Crucify him! Crucify him!"

The Resurrection takes its meaning from the Cross. The Cross and Resurrection are really one utterly transforming event, creating entirely new possibilities of life for us. The force of all the evil of the world meets the force of all the good in the world, and, as a coal is turned to diamond by the pressure of the earth, life itself is transformed. A flash of blinding light breaks forth that changes everything forever.

What did the Resurrection mean to the disciples? Unimaginable joy, of course, but also puzzlement and fear. Jesus tells them explicitly to be witnesses of what they have seen. They must have wondered, "How can we do that? Who will believe us?" And maybe: "Will they not kill us too?"

In fact the forces of evil will kill them. Tradition tells us that all of the apostles except John ended their lives at the hand of murderous violence.

It is also true—though they do not know it yet—that having given them this command to be witnesses, Jesus will leave them, returning to his Father in heaven.

So: did the Resurrection really change everything, as they hoped, or did it change nothing at all? They acted on the faith and hope that it changed everything, but they must also have been afraid that it did not.

We can ask about ourselves: What does the Resurrection mean to us? Has it changed everything—or nothing? Has Jesus abandoned us, leaving us just as we were before he came?

The answer to the last question is surely no. Jesus is with us, and we can know him in many ways. For example:

—Jesus is present in the Gospel, as a unique voice constantly exhorting us, puzzling and confounding us, challenging our deepest thoughts and expectations. *"Sell all you have and give the money to the poor," "I come not to bring peace but a sword," "The first shall be last and the last shall be first."* In this living, and often upsetting, voice that we hear every Sunday, the one who was dead is now alive.

—Jesus is present in the Church. He is present in this room, with us and among us. *"When two or three are gathered in my name, I am there among them"* (Matthew 18:20). We can actually see Jesus' presence in the love and generosity and faithfulness we behold in those around us, in this and other churches, of all denominations. In no other place can these things be found in this way. Here, in his Church, the one who was dead is now alive.

—Jesus is present in other people, especially suffering people, and in our response to them. When we confront suffering we can let the force and light of his love shine in us, as we sometimes do; or we can, as we also sometimes do, close our hearts to him and to the suffering before us. Sometimes maybe we can even say, in a phrase from one of George Herbert's poems, that Christ "is not dead but lives in me." (George Herbert, "Aaron.") The one who was dead is now alive.

—Jesus is also present in the Eucharist. I know there have historically been different theologies about this, but I believe that Jesus is present in that moment and I think you do too. I certainly don't think we are just remembering him. In the Eucharist the one who was dead is now alive.

Jesus is present to us in other ways as well, but I want to focus on one that is especially hard to describe: he is present in our deepest sense of what life itself is, what its meaning is, what we can at the center of our souls hope for, what we need not fear. Somehow the cosmic squeezing of evil against good that produced the Cross and the Resurrection has generated something new, something alive in us and among us—a different sense of life itself.

A part of what I mean is the sense that love and truth and goodness are real possibilities for us. We can hope for them, we can work for them, despite all the evil that exists in the world and in ourselves.

For the classical philosophers who wrote before Jesus' time it was a real question why we should strive to be good, to be faithful, and kind, and devoted to others. These things will not make us rich, or powerful, or famous, or safe; they will not add to our prestige, or make people defer to us. They will in all likelihood not even be known to the world at all. So why do them?

Yet look at what you yourselves actually do. You care for a sick and dying person, perhaps someone who has lost much of his or her mind, and you do it with love and attention and care. Or you teach special education students who will never be able to function normally in the world, and you do it with love and attention and care. Or you just treat others with kindness and respect, even when it is hard to do so. Or you admit to a friend a way in which you have injured or betrayed him.

Why do you do these things? Who knows what you do? Maybe no one knows. There is no reward. Why do you do them?

I think you know the answer. I think the reason you do these things is that the one who was dead is now alive, present in you and me and in the world. He has shown us that hope and meaning are possible in a cruel world, and that failure in the end does not matter. What matters is the effort we make of love and care and devotion. It does not matter that no one knows what we do; it does not matter how much we do; it does not matter if we fail. What matters is who we are, and whether we are striving to live our lives out of truth and love.

Because of the Resurrection, we live not in the light of this world—the world of money and power and consequence, the world whose rewards turn to ashes in the mouth—but in the light of another world, a world in which the meaning of what we do, and what we are, is not dependent upon being seen and recognized by others. Those things are not part of the economy of this world. The world in whose light we live is one in which Jesus knows our hearts and our striving for what they are. His knowledge and love and forgiveness make possible a new life, with a new meaning.

We all know people who seem to have lost all meaning in life. Nothing they do has value. Everything is a source of despair. Maybe they self-consciously propound a philosophy that declares the emptiness of human life and value. But then they find someone to love, someone who loves them—maybe a spouse or partner, maybe a friend, maybe a child, maybe a kindred soul across generations—and all is changed. None of the old questions is real. It does not matter that we shall die. We have love, we have life. That is all we shall want or need.

So it is with the Resurrection. It changes life from the inside out. Now our every act, our every effort, has meaning, the meaning that comes from reciprocal love: our love for him, his love for us.

He is life itself. His Resurrection is his and our victory over death.

Amen

To someone outside the Church the whole idea of the Resurrection is likely to sound bizarre. Of course we cannot fully know what the Resurrection was, or is, but we affirm our belief in it whenever we repeat one of the major creeds of the Church. What are we doing when we do that?

Here we face a special instance of what might be called the general problem of religious language. Sometimes religious language, even our own, sounds disconnected from experience or reality, like a string of empty phrases and clichés. It can seem abstract and conclusory, very hard to connect to our own lives, and authoritarian too, in the sense that we are expected to use it, whether or not we understand it or have made it in a real way our own. This problem is especially acute where the language affirms something that does not make sense in ordinary terms, such as the Resurrection itself.

It is true that the language of our religion, including the language of Resurrection, can be used in dead and empty ways. But perhaps there are other possibilities. Can we ourselves use it in a way that is full of meaning and life and truth, so that it is not authoritarian, but deeply respectful of individual responsibility and experience (both our own and other people's); so that it is not overconfident and conclusory, but aware of its own limitations, connected to other ways of speaking, and open to what lies beyond language, within the self and in the world?

Can we use it in a way that makes it, not a language in which it is impossible to tell the truth, but a language that is able to tell the truth above all truths?

Table of Gospel Readings

Gospel citation	Chapter	Title	Lectionary citation
Matthew 13:1–9, 18–23	9	Parable of the Sower	Proper 10 A
Matthew 13:31–33, 44–49	24	The Mustard Seed	Proper 12 A
Matthew 16:13–20	25	"Who Do You Say I Am?"	Proper 16 A
Matthew 16:21–27	10	"Get Thee Behind Me, Satan"	Proper 17 A
Matthew 18:21–35	26	"Seventy Times Seven"	Proper 19 A
Matthew 20:1–16	11	The Laborers in the Vineyard	Proper 20 A
Mark 1:40–45	27	Healing the Leper	Epiphany 6 B
Mark 6:7–13	14	Sending out the Twelve	Proper 10 B
Mark 6:45–52	5	Walking on Water	Proper 12 B
Mark 9:2–8	12	The Transfiguration	Last Epiphany B
Luke 3:1–6	16	"Prepare the Way of the Lord"	Advent 2 C
Luke 10:1–12, 16–20	18	Sending the Seventy	Proper 9 C
Luke 10:25–37	6	The Good Samaritan	Proper 10 C
Luke 12:32–40	19	"Sell Your Possessions"	Proper 14 C
Luke 13:22–30	7	The Narrow Door	Proper 16 C
Luke 15:1–10	20	The Lost Sheep, the Lost Coin	Proper 19 C
Luke 16:19–31	3	Lazarus and the Rich Man	Proper 21 C

Gospel citation	Chapter	Title	Lectionary citation
Luke 18:9–14	21	The Pharisee and the Tax Collector	Proper 25 C
Luke 24:36–49	29	The Resurrection	Easter 3 B
John 3:1–16	2	Nicodemus	Lent 2 A
John 6:60–69	15	"To Whom Can We Go?"	Proper 16 B
John 10:1–10	22	The Good Shepherd	Easter 4A
John 12:20–33	28	The Grain of Wheat	Lent 5B
John 14:15–21	23	"You in Me, and I in You"	Easter 6A
John 15:9–17	1	"Love One Another'	Easter 6B
John 18:1—19:42	8, 13	The Passion	Good Friday ABC
John 20:19–31	4	Doubting Thomas	Easter 2 ABC
John 21:1–14	17	Jesus on the Beach	Easter 3 C

www.ingramcontent.com/pod-product-compliance
Lightning Source LLC
Chambersburg PA
CBHW070314230426
43663CB00011B/2130